As for Me and My House

Dolores Hayford

CREATION
HOUSE

BOOKS ABOUT SPIRIT-LED LIVING
ORLANDO, FLORIDA

Creation House
Strang Communications Company
600 Rinehart Road
Lake Mary, FL 32746
Phone: (800) 283-8494
Fax: (407) 333-7100

First printing, June 1995
Second printing, September 1995

This guidebook to help parents teach their children the principles of Scripture is lovingly dedicated to the memory of my dear friend, Dorothy Winter.

Dorothy had a great burden for families. Aware of the moral decay eating away at the Christian standards established by the founding fathers of our nation, she gave everything she had to alert parents to this truth: Re-establishing these principles can only be accomplished within the family as children see them lived out with blessing .The organization she established, American Family Services, continues to minister to families across the nation — a living, vital memorial to a godly woman.

Because Dorothy believed — as do I — in the power of God's Word to "tame the old nature and convert the soul," she asked me to share some of the ways we interested our children in the Bible. I can attest to the value of the time we invested in sharing the things of the Lord with our kids.

It was never our goal to make ministers of them, and they know that. I recall my husband, a railroad man, once telling the boys: "I don't care what profession you choose as long as you are God's man in that profession."

Because our kids grew up enjoying the Word of God and discussing it with us, they are teaching it to their own children. I now have nine grandchildren and sixteen great-grandchildren who are happy and contented in Christ.

As it happened, all three of our children went into full-time ministry. Jack, our eldest, is the senior pastor of the Church on the Way in Van Nuys, California, a Foursquare church. He has been used to minister to pastors of many denominations around the world and has authored many widely acclaimed books, both for ministers and for the church.

Our second son, Jim, pastored successfully for many years and is serving as director of leadership development and church growth for the International Church of the Foursquare Gospel.

Our daughter, Luanne Chumley, with her husband, Duanne, served on the mission field in Hong Kong. She went to be with the Lord at age thirty-nine.

Of our nine grandchildren, five are in full-time ministry. Two of the great-grandchildren have already announced that they are headed in the same direction. (Most of them are too young to be giving thought to a vocation yet, but six-year-old Jack IV has been heard preaching to his teddy bears in the basement of his parents' home.)

It is my firm conviction, as it was Dorothy's, that this can be the heritage of any family who will recognize the power of God's Word to captivate the hearts of children if it is properly presented.

Contents

Foreword

*H*ow ironic can a situation be? Here I am, introducing to you the person who introduced me to the world. Please meet my mother — Dolores Hayford.

More than anything else I'd like to tell you about her is that I know you'd love her if you had the opportunity to meet her in person. My mamma is *bright* (at seventy-nine and years before!), she's *interesting* (and if she doesn't know the subject that interests you, she'll learn it!), and she's *fun to be with* (as her children, grandchildren, great-grandchildren and numberless friends will tell you!).

She's also godly. But don't invest in any monastic notions about that word when it applies to Mamma. Her godliness isn't reflected in any religious pretensions or stylized spirituality. She simply loves the Lord and lives out that love. Really.

And she's been doing this all my life — genuinely taking the Lord seriously, caring for people that others didn't seem willing to take time for, and teaching, speaking, writing and generally "touching people for God" every way she can (even though she's not formally in public ministry).

Most and best of all, she's been a mother. A very good one.

Besides loving my dad with all her heart (he went home to glory a few years ago) and keeping our home a happy place to live in, visit and be around, Mamma raised three kids. Even though none of us was taught or required to think that "being in the ministry" was a profession superior to any other, all of us yielded our lives to the full-time service of our Lord Jesus Christ. No matter how you measure it, Mamma had something to do with it. She made serving God a practical, sensible and joyous way of life — something you'd like to do, and help others know how to do as well.

My brother, Jim, has been a pastor for thirty years (he's now a leader at the headquarters of the Foursquare church, helping other pastors advance their effectiveness in ministry and church growth).

My sister, Luanne, was a missionary to Hong Kong and a zealous intercessor until her home-going in 1978. And I'm just starting my fortieth year as a preacher and teacher of God's Word.

All of us would chalk up the blessings and privileges of our lives and ministries to the grace of

God. But then, we'd each probably add — "who worked so much in us through Mamma." She has prayed for us all with incredible sensitivity and discernment. (At times she came to me with "something the Lord showed me," and I found out God wouldn't let me get away with anything. The Almighty kept "telling my mother" on me!)

She raised us God's way, but she didn't do it alone. My dad was in the military as a young man, then was a railroad man most of my life. Both professions bred a man with a solid mix of authority and responsibility, which were relayed with a fervor for "doing things right, even if no one's looking." We kids knew we were loved, and we grew up learning in a house where God's truth was the rule, but His love was the mood. Holy living was made both happy and livable.

I have lots of stories about Mamma's special instances of influencing me such as:

The time she dreamed Jesus met her on a darkened hillside where burnt brush had removed vital growth. Daddy said after dinner one night, "Honey, tell the kids what you told me about the Lord's 'word' to you."

The word: "Daughter, it is too late for you to be walking among the barren places."

The impact: a sudden recognition that it was time to shape up any loose edges in my own lifestyle, because if God was cautioning my *Mom*, then we were all in trouble!

Or the time shortly after I'd finished my studies for ministry: I was standing in the kitchen conversing with Mamma, when she casually turned to me to say: "Son, whatever you do in ministry, just never forget one thing: None of us has a corner on truth." I haven't forgotten. And I haven't any idea how that one word of wisdom — gently laid on a young just-graduated-from-theological-school pastor — has kept me relatively free from petty attitudes toward other parts of Christ's body and has helped me steer clear of provincialism or doctrinaire divisiveness.

Mamma is a dear lady. But notwithstanding my obvious reasons for being judged as prejudiced, I'll go further: She's a great lady. I think you'll get a small taste of why I say that as you read and use this book — an example of how her good sense makes holiness livable and godliness happy.

In this book, the way is pointed toward raising a family God's way. That's no stilted claim: You can believe it, because my mother has done it, and she keeps on influencing others to do the same. Though crowding eighty, she is still invited by young parents to teach classes on parenting, and with good reason. She has proven the plan God's Word reveals. And she relates it in ways that are so "just-plain-good-sense" in their delivery — you not only agree with her, you also believe you can do it too.

We learned some of it from her, and all of my

kids are living examples of Jesus at work in a family — with a raft of grandchildren coming up now the same way.

Yep! You'll like Dolores Hayford. Just like I do — besides loving her as my Mamma.

Jack W. Hayford, pastor
The Church on the Way
Van Nuys, California

*A Mandate
For Parenting*

*H*ow many times have you begun family devotions only to fail at making it a part of your life? Why is it that we just can't seem to "make it fly"? Do you remember when you and your spouse decided to have devotions together before you had a family? How long did it take to fizzle out? A couple of months (or weeks, or days)? I remember those failures all too well!

Parents can leave no greater heritage than a new generation solidly planted in Christ. It is only in retrospect that we recognize the long-term importance of parenting. As our children become independent, unique individuals, we come to see that their integrity, their choice of a mate and even their approach to parenting has been shaped largely by the seeds we have sown. Whether by training or by ignorant neglect, these early formative years make all the difference!

If we hope to meet God's mandate to parents, there must be a consistent sharing of God's Word with our children.

My husband and I discovered that it takes more than prayer and Bible reading to develop in children an appreciation for spiritual values. To be lasting, it will have to be enjoyable. It can also be the greatest learning experience of your life — it was for our family. Discussing the Word of God with your kids *is* fun!

I am going to share a workable plan with you. It is God's simple, direct plan, set forth in His Word with explicit directions. It is a command, but it comes to us underscored by an impassioned cry from the heart of God. It is God's tri-fold mandate for parenting:

> [1] *You shall love the Lord your God with all your heart, with all your soul, and with all your strength. And these words which I command you today shall be in your heart.* [2] *You shall teach them diligently to your children, and* [3] *shall talk of them when you sit in your house, when you walk by the way, when you lie down, and when you rise up (Deut. 6:4-7).*

God's mandate for parenting tells parents how to establish a family in intimate relationship with God.

We need to know:

1. What our relationship with Him is sup-posed to be.

2. What we are to teach our children.

3. How, when and where we are to do this.

Consider the handwriting on our national walls. The moral state of America is the result of disap-pearing standards once set by the families of our nation. Parents have become so wrapped up in getting "their piece of the pie" that the pantry has run out of staples! Clothes, toys, personal TVs, computers, video games and cars — these things do not make a child feel loved. Giving ourselves — the spending of time — this is what they truly want. Parental influence outweighs all else in the shaping of a child's life. God planned it that way.

If you are overwhelmed with the responsibilities of parenting, take heart. God never asks more of us than we are able to deliver. He is not trying to strong-arm us into becoming His kind of people. The simple truth is that we were created to be like Him. We function best in those areas where we have allowed Him to have preeminence. It makes sense that the Manufacturer knows how to get the best use out of His product, right?

God's Word acknowledges human frailty (Ps. 103:4).

God deals with the attitudes of our hearts (1 Sam. 16:7). The heart that is hoping, yearning, wanting, striving or longing to be all that God commanded is a "perfect heart" (2 Chron. 16:9). This heart is grieved when failure occurs. It is quick to repent. God is pleased with such a heart (Ps. 51:17).

Abraham had such a heart. Though at times he failed God, God dealt with his heart — not his performance. God called Abraham "the apple of his eye" (Deut. 32:10). The New Testament refers to him as "the friend of God" (James 2:23). This is good news for us, and it is something we must convey to our children. We, and they, will fail at times. But if we come to our Father in true repentance, He not only will forgive us, He also will cleanse us from the guilt of our failure. He erases the record!

Understanding these important truths will turn His directives into challenges that each of us can rise to meet with true confidence. God is on our side. He delights in our desire to please Him.

When Moses received the Ten Commandments from God on Mount Sinai, he went back down the mountain and delivered God's words to the children of Israel. Although the people saw the cloud of God's glory and heard His voice, they responded by saying:

> *We have seen this day that God speaks with man...If we hear the voice of the Lord our God anymore, then we shall die...You*

*go near and hear all that the Lord Our
God may say, and tell us all that the Lord
our God says to you, and we will hear and
do it (Deut. 5:24-25, 27).*

God was offering them a "road map," but the
condition of their own hearts was making them
afraid, like too many of us to this day. They wanted a "go-between." So they pleaded with Moses,
whom they revered as a holy man: "You speak
with Him! Whatever He commands, we will do!"
From the time of Adam (who hid from God
because he had been disobedient) until this very
moment, whenever man falls short of what he
knows he is to be, he hides behind an excuse.

God sent His Son to provide a way for us to
become a part of His family. Our sense of inade-
quacy seems to us a legitimate excuse to "let someone else do it." Getting out there in the workplace
to get our share of the manna separates us from
rich personal learning time with our Father.

God longs for a one-on-one relationship with us.
We, like the Israelites, occupy a pew on Sunday,
expecting our "holy man" to teach us. God will never
force us into a relationship of intimacy, but hear
His passion as He speaks to Moses:

*Oh, that they had such a heart in them
that they would fear Me and always keep
all My commandments, that it might be*

17

*well with them and with their children
forever! (Deut. 5:29).*

Our children will put the same importance on intimacy with God that we demonstrate before them. It is imperative that we lead our children into an understanding of a truly righteous but very understanding God. We, and they, need to sense His Father-heart toward us and realize the value He places upon us as individuals and as a family. *We need to help them recognize that every directive He gives us is a personal blessing for us.* These are principles that will enhance life. They affect both our physical and our spiritual well-being. What a challenge it is to instill this vision for our children's own lives.

I hope I have whetted your appetite. Kids learn best by what they see and by repetition. It gives them a sense of importance and self-worth to discuss these things with us. This happy and fruitful experience will develop a lifetime habit that they will continue in some form with their children after them.

So — this is not your average devotional guide. It is a simple sharing of many of the things that my husband and I did with our children, and they with theirs, that has borne fruit.

This book is intended to help you fulfill the parental charge given in Deuteronomy 6:6-7. It will help your children understand the loving nature of God, and He will play a major role in their lives.

If This Plan Is To Succeed

(Some absolutes from
the author to the parent.)

- Ask your older children to help you make this a family affair. The smaller children need the acceptance and encouragement and praise of their older brothers and sisters.

- Be sure each family member (even nonreaders) has a Bible. The memory verses should be underlined and dated in the margin when properly "owned."

- Allow your children who read fairly well to read the Scripture portion each day. Express your appreciation for their help.

- Parent, this is of utmost importance: Read the lesson through before you meet with your family. Teach it in your own way. Revise the discussion questions to suit your family's circumstances.

- Move the lesson ahead when the older ones are ready. The younger children will catch up during review times.

- Have the children take turns opening each session with prayer, primarily to thank God for His willingness to teach your family His Word. Welcome Him as your teacher (Ps. 25:12). Talk to your children about the awesomeness of the Creator wanting to take time to teach us.

- Where there are two parents in the home, the father should direct each session.

- Each lesson starts with prayer suggestions for the child who is praying. Emphasize that this is a time that God draws near, by His Spirit, to help us understand His truth.

NOTE TO READERS

Whenever you see the ▶ symbol in this devotional guide, the text immediately following the symbol will be instructional material to explain or guide you in the presentation of that particular unit of study.

Week 1

God Wants Us To Love and Obey Him

Memory Verse

Oh, that there was such a heart in them that they would fear Me and always keep all My commandments, that it might be well with them and with their children forever!

Deuteronomy 5:29

Goal
To see God as a loving, caring Father.

Prayer Focus
Thank God for His great love and concern for *our* family. He wants to teach us (Ps. 35:10).

▶ Allow your children time to think about their answers to your discussion questions. With encouragement it won't be long until they jump right in during discussion periods. Enthusiasm, sharing and brevity are essential to maintain your child's interest throughout the year.

Unit 1

*How God
Feels About Us*

(▶ Read Deuteronomy 5:29 with feeling, but don't comment yet.) Ask: "How do you think God was feeling when He spoke these words?"

The memory verse for this week shows us something wonderful about God.

Do you remember the first word in the verse? It is the word "Oh!" That word tells us something special about God.

"Oh!" expresses many different feelings. I have a list of some of the ways we feel when we say "Oh!" Can you tell me the feeling that each sentence expresses? (▶ Let your children respond after each statement.)

Oh! What beautiful flowers! What a nice
    thing to do! *(Joy)*
Oh, this tooth hurts so badly! *(Pain)*

Oh, I'm so sorry you cut your finger!
  (Sympathy)
Oh dear! I can't imagine why they are so
  late! *(Anxiety)*
Oh, you make me so mad! *(Anger)*
Oh, I'm so sorry I said that! *(Regret)*
Oh! You are such a wonderful friend to
  me! *(Love)*

Let's listen again to how God felt when He said
"Oh." (▶ Read Deuteronomy 5:29 out loud again.)

God loves His people dearly! He wants us to
learn His Laws so we will choose to do right and
won't get into trouble. He wants us to have a
happy home. He wants us to care for one another.

It is love that causes parents to create rules for
their children (▶ Explain briefly). And it is love that
causes children to obey the rules their parents have
given to them. We are going to find out what the
Bible says about families and talk about God's love
— and His rules. We will also talk about our love
for each other and about the family rules that create our happy home.

Together we will discover that God has provided our family with all the guidelines we need for a
happy life. He loves us so much that He wants
everything to go well in our home, and He tells us
how to make that happen.

► *Parent Tip*

Have a "chatty" review at the beginning of each session. "What did we talk about last time?" "Who remembers....?" Review is a way to develop in your children an inexhaustible delight in talking about God and His Word. It should be a daily part of your time together. It takes many days to plant each new Bible truth securely.

Take time (perhaps even one session) before you begin each new unit to discuss all aspects of your previous study. Stimulate your family's thinking with questions and responses of your own. Let your children present the Bible thought in their own conversational style.

There are several ways to make this time interesting and fun. Use the participation chart in the back of this book to award points for your children's contributions to the review time. Don't let your kids think that you are checking up on them. Instead find ways to turn the review time into a game, with rewards for participation. You may want to use their favorite food as a reward. Another option is to allow children to earn a special toy or activity for getting a certain number of points..

Ask questions of all your children to ensure that everyone has the opportunity to respond. Encourage your children to enlarge on the Bible truths, adapting them to your own particular family situations.

Unit 2

Love God — Heart, Soul and Strength

Our memory verse tells us God longs for His people to fear Him and to keep His commandments. God loves us — our own special family!

He wants us to have a happy home. He wants us to care for one another. And He wants us to love and trust Him more than anything or anyone else.

Remember, earlier we read God's charge about total commitment:

> *You shall love the Lord your God with all your heart, with all your soul, and with all your strength (Deut. 6:4).*

Those are the three kinds of true devotion He wants from us. Our heart is the seat of our emotions; if we love Him, we make it His home. Our soul controls our feelings and behavior. As we love God more and more, He gives us strength to refuse temptation.

That's loving God with all our heart, soul and strength. Our hearts of love cause us to use all our strength to control our actions.

We will still do wrong things sometimes. Many times we get in trouble because we break a rule or a law. For example, you may fail a test in school because you did not study for it. Or a jaywalker may be hit by a passing car because he disregarded traffic laws.

Cheating on study time or traffic laws will be forgiven, but there is always a price to pay. We will still get an *F* on that test, and the jaywalker may have to suffer with a broken leg.

What are some of the things you might do that would result in discipline? Discipline is part of the process of discipling. It helps us remember *not* to do that same thing again. It helps us remember what is right and why it is right. It teaches us to "shape up!"

Discipline becomes less necessary as we let Jesus rule in our hearts.

▶ *Parent Tip*

As disciplining occasions arise, review with the child why discipline is part of the process of discipling. Discipline is caring enough to make disobedience uncomfortable — something remembered well enough to avoid repeat performances.

Ask questions from the lessons. Make favorable comments about each child's contribution. Lead smaller children to complete their partial answers. Give your children opportunities to recite the memory verses (marking on a chart the name of each child who does a perfect job, if you are using that additional method in your time together).

DISCUSSION QUESTIONS

(▶ Always express questions in ways your children will understand. Be sure they feel confident about their responses.)

Can you think of a time when you were saved from possible danger because you obeyed the instructions of a parent or teacher?

How can we demonstrate love for God in the way we behave?

What three parts of us were created to love God?

Of the three ways we are to love God, which part deals with our behavior?

What are the three ways we should love God according to Deuteronomy 5:29?

Unit 3

Godly Fear
Is Proof of a Wise Heart

Have you ever been afraid to confess that you have done something wrong? Even when we know we will be forgiven, we still dread the discipline we can expect because of our disobedience.

It is the same way with God's law. That same dread or fear of what's going to happen is the kind of fear God is talking about in our memory verse when He says:

> *Oh, that there was such a heart in them that they would fear Me (Deut. 5:29).*

Let me give an example. One of God's laws is "Do not tell lies." He made that law because He knows how much trouble lying will cause. At first we fear someone will discover the lie. Sometimes we even tell a second lie to try to cover up the first one. Finally, the truth comes out, and we are in trouble!

The worst part of the trouble is not the discipline we receive; it is the fact that people doubt what we say. Because we lied to them before, they don't know when we are telling the truth. The person may forgive us, and God does too, but we know how they feel, and we hurt inside.

Also, if we do not confess it, the guilt in our heart makes us unhappy. It hardens our hearts. Sin separates us from God, and it becomes easier to disobey God's rules again. He wants us to keep His commandments so we will have clean and happy hearts. He wants us to fear what sin can do.

God doesn't want us to be afraid of Him. The trouble that comes as a result of breaking God's laws is the thing He wants us to fear. God loves us. He wants us to love Him. He gave us rules to live by, because He knew obedience would bring us happiness.

Just think — we will always do right when we are at home in heaven. When we know God's Word, we know *why* we should or should not do certain things. We know when we disobey, we are crowding Him out of our heart. Aren't you glad we will always do right after we are in heaven with Him? Be thankful for parents who correct persistent disobedience. And remember — it is the *result* of disobedience we should fear, not discipline alone.

DISCUSSION QUESTIONS

Why does God want us to be aware of the consequences of disobedience?

Does discipline motivate us to keep His commandments?

Can you tell me in one word how guilt makes you feel?

Can you think of a personal experience to share with us that shows how obedience can bring happiness?

In what area of your life have you been trying to learn to be more obedient?

▶ *Parent Tip*

Get your smaller children ready to be tucked into bed immediately after family devotions. This frees you to spend special time praying with the older kids during their bedtime. These lessons are the "sit-down" times of Deuteronomy 6:7. The bedtime prayers and talks are the "when you lie on your bed" times.

Unit 4

God's Rules
In My Heart

Children's Prayer Focus

Ask God for a desire to put His rules in our hearts.

While we are here on earth, all who receive Jesus as Savior become a part of God's family—we join His army. Obeying God's rules will help us to defeat Satan's attempts to keep us from serving God.

When you really love someone, you want to do the things that please that person. It pleases God when we give Him our hearts and walk in His ways.

The things we have studied in these first few days have shown us how much God loves us. He wants us to love Him just as much. But Satan tries very hard to make us ignore God's rules.

Putting God's rules in our hearts will help us to avoid the troubles that come to people who are disobedient. God wants us to make the right choices in our lives.

We have seen that although He gives us careful directives, He never forces us to keep His rules. That is something we must choose to do. That's why our hearts must have a desire to please Him.

As we choose correctly, He blesses our lives. He gives us special gifts. He makes our lives fruitful as we grow in obedience. He is making us ready to be a part of His "forever family" in heaven.

When someone builds a house, a lot of work takes place before the walls go up. The ground must be leveled, and the concrete foundation must be laid. The Bible tells us, "For no other foundation can anyone lay than that which is laid, which is Jesus Christ" (1 Cor. 3:11). God knew we were not able to stand alone, so He gave His Son to live in us and to be our firm foundation — our strength.

God's rules are like the strong boards — the walls we build on the foundation by our obedience. When the storms of life appear, such a life will remain standing. With Christ we can do all things (Phil. 4:13).

▶ *Parent Tip*

Read each lesson thoroughly and then discuss it with your children. They will enjoy participating in a conversation about what God has said to the people He loves.

DISCUSSION QUESTIONS

What are some of the troubles that you could experience? How can you avoid them?

What is the most important decision we face in life?

What is the strong foundation for our lives that will stand forever?

Can you name some of the rules that God gave us to obey?

Unit 5

Making Right Choices

Our lesson today is a special story about making right choices.

One evening, a newspaper delivery boy missed one of the houses where he was supposed to leave a paper. The Christian father in that family enjoyed reading his paper, and he knew just what time to expect the delivery. He looked for it several times and was more displeased each time he found the porch empty. When he came back into the house the third time, he slammed the door very hard. When the mother rushed out of the kitchen, the frustrated father asked: "What's the matter with you? Can't I close my own front door without you running in to check on me?"

In his heart he knew he was being unkind. He was ashamed, and he tried to cover up his unkindness by saying: "That dumb kid who delivers the paper is goofing off someplace. Fooling around with his friends, I suppose!"

The mother said: "Perhaps everyone's paper is late today. I'll call the office and see if there is a problem."

"I'll do it myself. You get dinner!" the father said rather crossly.

The people at the newspaper office were unaware of any problem with the delivery of the papers that day. The father dialed the home of the paper boy, but the telephone line was busy. After three unsuccessful tries, he banged the receiver down angrily.

His daughter saw that he was upset. "What's wrong, Dad?" she asked.

"Nothing that you can do anything about! It's that dumb kid that was supposed to be here an hour ago with my paper. Don't bother me — I have to make a phone call." The girl walked away, hurt and angered by her father's unpleasant words.

The father finally reached the paper boy's mother by phone. "Is your son home from his route yet?" he asked rudely.

Sensing the man's bad mood, she replied cautiously, "Why...yes, he is. Is something wrong, sir?"

"I'm one of his regular customers," he said. "I want to speak to him!"

What do you think the father *will* say to the boy? What do you think he *should* say? (▶ Get responses from your children.)

We have learned that Christians sometimes behave badly. This father was having a time like that. One of the reasons why God wants us to keep His commandments is that so many people are made unhappy when we do not act the way we should! It's not just our anger that hurts others. Jealousy, envy and lying begin deep inside of us, in our hearts! No wonder we feel miserable. We are crowding Jesus out of our hearts — the home we gave to Him.

The father in our story needed to apologize and ask the people he hurt to forgive him. But it was also very important for him to talk to his heavenly Father about it! He will also forgive, but we need to ask Him to help us remember His laws before we hurt others with our disobedience.

Learning to hear God's voice and to make right choices will help us overcome our disobedience.

▶ *Parent Tip*

These lessons do not need to be finished in one day. Take as much time as is needed for each child to grasp the lesson truth. Some lessons will take less time, others more. This is not a race to be run or a book to be finished. It is the establishing of a family fellowship in the Word of God.

Week 2

Joining God's Army

Memory Verse

*You shall love the Lord your God
with all your heart, with all your soul,
and with all your strength.*

Deuteronomy 6:5

Goal

To understand the importance of learning to express love and care for God and for family members.

Prayer Focus

Show your children that the words of Deuteronomy 6:5 were directed to parents first. God wanted children to see how and why their parents loved God so much. Thank God for parents and pray for the parents' needs.

▶ Try to instill a desire in the older children to assist the younger family members. The world is full of families (Christian families among them!) whose children are kinder to their school friends than they are to their own brothers and sisters.

Unit 1

Our Commanding Officer

When the United States Army sets up an operation in another country, the first duty for the commanding officer is to set up a command post from which all the decisions, plans and activities for the entire operation are mapped out and prepared.

When God sent His Son to earth, He sent Him to win a battle. Satan, our enemy, thought he had won this battle when Christ died on the cross at Calvary. But Jesus went right into the devil's territory and won a great victory, freeing all the captives of death who had been waiting for their Messiah. This proved His lordship over heaven and earth.

When we invite Jesus into our lives, He becomes our commanding officer and sets up a command post within our hearts. The Bible tells us about God's command post; today we will see what the psalmist David had to say about it.

These are characteristics of the heart as found in the book of Psalms:

1. Desire to praise God wholeheartedly (9:1). Tell of one "marvelous" work He has done toward you.

2. A heart that hears and immediately obeys (27:8). What might your heart "hear"?

3. A heart that tries to hide sin (66:18). "Regard" means to honor and esteem.

4. A happy heart, full of praise (28:7). What caused this joyful state to occur?

5. A heart God desires to honor (37:4). How can we win God's honor?

6. A heart that lives by God's law prevents "sliding" along the way (37:31). What do you think this means?

7. A heart that longs to be restored when a wrongdoing has occurred (51:10). Does this require repentance?

8. A heart that is established, mature and unafraid of the devil (112:8). This is our desire for each of you.

9. A heart hungry to please and to learn more about God (119:32).

10. A heart that is fighting the old nature (34:18). Read Philippians 3:13-14.

DISCUSSION QUESTIONS

What is one way that having Jesus in your heart is like being in an army?

Can you share a time in your life when you knew in your heart something Jesus wanted you to do?

What Scripture verse have you hidden in your heart that is especially meaningful to you? Why?

What more would you like to know about God?

Unit 2

Build a
Heritage of Godliness

Children's Prayer Focus

Thank God for the Christian heritage in your family.

The author of this book, together with her husband, built a heritage for their family that is a wonderful model for our own family.

Her family has proved the importance of teaching each family member to understand God and His Word. She and her husband faithfully laid a spiritual foundation by having daily talks with their children about God's principles.

▒ The Hayford Heritage ▒

As new converts, my husband and I attended a church where the pastor was a great Bible teacher and very family-oriented. He taught us that what our children became depended largely on what we modeled in the home, rather than our church attendance or the children's ministry within the church.

He encouraged us to study God's Word for ourselves. One day my husband read the passage in Deuteronomy that we have been dealing with in the lessons thus far:

You shall love the Lord your God with all your heart, with all your soul, and with all your strength. And these words which I command you today shall be in your heart. You shall teach them diligently to your children, and shall talk of them when you sit in your house, when you walk by the way, when you lie down, and when you rise up (6:5-7).

"Here it is!" he called excitedly. "This is how we are supposed to raise the kids — we are supposed to teach them God's ways." He paused, then continued: "But it must be fun Mrs. (his pet name for me). We have to think of a way to make it fun!"

We started by simply telling a story from the Bible. With our first child, Jack, we dramatized the story of Abraham. "Can you imagine, Jack," we asked, "how fearful it must have been for Abraham? He had to leave everyone he knew. He didn't even know where he was going! What kind of animals do you think were out there? Do you think he met other people?"

We elaborated on the names and characters

in the story. One night my husband said: "That story was put in the Bible for the Hayford family. God wants us to learn to trust Him when there are hard things we have to do. He told us about His friend, Abraham, because He wants us to be His friends too!"

We also insisted the children know where a Bible story was located. That was a *must!*

Applying the Word where it was appropriate was a part of our daily life. The basis for our teaching has always been the mandate for parenting that God gave in Deuteronomy 6:5-7. There is no telling what hour of day or night a situation might arise that may prove to be the perfect time to teach a lifelong lesson.

I shared a verse of promise with the children before they left for school in the morning. At bedtime, we spent time with each child, discussing the day and praying with them.

We never suggested that our children pursue ministerial vocations. We did ask them to attend a Christian college for one year before they went on to a university. None of them ever transferred out of the Christian colleges, although some went on to achieve academic degrees from other colleges. All three of our children chose the ministry. Five of our grandchildren have done the same, and two of our great-grandchildren are already planning to enter the ministry.

Unit 3

Pray For
One Another

God designed the family to provide love and companionship for each family member. If we live by God's rules, it will make our home a place we like better than any other place in the world. It also makes other people want the kind of family life we have. That is one of the best ways to win others into God's army.

One of the ways our family can live in harmony is for both parent and child to be obedient to the rules that are given to each. One of these rules tells us: "Children, obey your parents" (Eph. 6:1). Do we always want to do what we are told to do? Why do parents insist that children do things in a pre-scribed way? (▶ Allow each child to make a contribution to this discussion.)

The love most parents have for their children is very deep. They loved them even before their birth. Nothing is more disappointing to a parent than rebellion on the part of a child. God says it must not be allowed. It must be followed with discipline.

When a child dishonors a parent with disobedience, that parent would be disobedient to God if he did not deal with it. Discipline proves to the child that he is important — and that his loving parents want him to do right. Children need and *want* boundaries, and they respect parents who set them.

God gave the command to parents to love Him wholeheartedly immediately after He gave them the ten commandments. He went on to say that these loving parents are to *diligently* teach His rules to their children.

Sometimes that involves discipline — and discipline is sometimes needed to help us learn God's ways.

Before discipline is administered, discussion should take place. Forgetfulness may be genuine, but it is not an excuse to overlook wrongdoing. Nor is it a loophole to be used to escape appropriate discipline.

Deliberate disobedience is rebellion and is totally unacceptable behavior.

DISCUSSION QUESTIONS

Do you feel that being disciplined has helped you learn self-control?

Are you happier when you know things have been made right between you and someone with whom you had a problem?

What behavior demands the strictest discipline?

Why should there be several different ways to discipline children?

(▶ The punishment should fit the crime.)

Unit 4

Appreciate Each Family Member's Uniqueness

God created each person to be unique, different from any other person. In our family, there are similarities that will be evident to those who know us. But each family member makes a unique contribution to our family. Each person is a special gift from God to this family.

Our author interviewed three siblings, ages three, seven and nine. Today we are going to see how these kids felt when asked to describe the good things about each other.

Nine-year-old Kevin said this about his seven-year-old sister: "She likes boy stuff enough to play with me." He ended his comments about his three-year-old brother by saying, "He is just a little kid, you know, but he can make me laugh. He is a real clown!"

Katie, speaking of her brothers, said: "I have two

brothers, a big one and a little one. My big brother is very smart, but he isn't stuck up if I don't know what he means about something. My little brother *is* a gift — we say that all the time because he is so cute!"

Sometimes kids feel like the youngest one is a real drag. But these children really enjoyed their little brother.

About the other two, the parent said: "Our nine-year-old is evidencing real ability to adapt alternatives. If a plan fails, he finds a solution. He has real organizational skills and leadership qualities. Our daughter has an exceptional ability to retain what you teach her about doing something, and requires of herself consistent improvement until it is right. Our little guy has remarkable mobile skills."

This was a family that recognized each member's special gifts. God wants our family to be able to do the same thing. His plan is for us to be a "lifetime support group" for one another.

Space limitations meant abbreviating the interview with the family just mentioned, but the attitudes their children evidence, and their seeming excitement over the projects they get involved in, are admirable.

It is certainly true (and valuable in the development of the children) that these two parents are aware of abilities that are surfacing in their children.

The mother of those three children grew up in a

home where both parents worked. They were not uncaring, but neither were they well-managed. She described her life as "living in a boat with five holes and four corks." She says, "We were always trying to move the corks around, hoping to let the least amount of water in. I have a real feeling for art, but my folks just thought art was something you did for fun. They would tell me, 'You're never going to get anywhere that way...there's no money in that!'" (You should see her paintings!)

Their father had been a foster child. "Not necessarily abused," he said, "but no one ever seemed to understand my need to take things apart to see how they worked." He is a mechanic who owns his own business now.

What special gifts have you been able to observe in each family member? (▶ Spend some time allowing each child to give his or her comments about each member of the family.)

Conclude by thanking God for the unique gifts within your family. Thank Him for choosing to put you together as a family.

Unit 5

Determination Is Our Strength

Children's Prayer Focus

Invite the Holy Spirit to teach us how to love God with all our strength.

Our memory verse continues by saying, "You shall love the Lord your God...with all your strength."

Do you remember Superman? He was a character named Clark Kent that always empowered himself with superhuman strength just when he needed strength most. Any time someone's safety was threatened by a power bigger than Clark Kent, he went through a metamorphosis and became Superman.

That is not the way we get our strength. By listening to our Commander, and asking for His strength to help us, we can be prepared to stand against anything the devil tries to do. The devil is afraid of those who know the promises of God and live by God's Word.

That strength is in us because Jesus is in us. "I can do all things through Christ who strengthens me" (Phil. 4:13). Loving God with all our strength will give us Jesus's determination to be pleasing to God. We won't be pulled in two different directions, yielding to the temptation to sin, and at the same time trying to pretend that we are really serving God. Our love for God will make us determined to serve only Him.

The Bible refers to a person who sometimes pleases God and sometimes yields to the devil's temptations as a "double-minded" man who is "unstable in all his ways" (James 1:8). The Bible warns us about our walk with God by saying:

> *No one can serve two masters; for either he will hate the one and love the other, or else he will be loyal to the one and despise the other. You cannot serve God and mammon (Matt. 6:24).*

It is by turning to Jesus that we become strong against temptation. The apostle Paul demonstrated this superhuman strength when he stated:

> *Brethren, I do not count myself to have apprehended; but one thing I do, forgetting those things which are behind and reaching forward to those things which are ahead, I press toward the goal for the prize of the upward call of God in Christ Jesus (Phil. 3:13-14).*

DISCUSSION QUESTIONS

Can you think of a time when you determined to do the right thing even though it was hard? Describe your feelings.

In what area of your life would you like to be like Superman and overcome something that is tempting you to do wrong?

What does it mean to love God "with all your strength"?

From where do we get the strength to serve God?

What could happen to us if we do not love God with all our strength?

God Is...

Memory Verse

*Who is the man [or person] that fears
the Lord? Him shall He teach
in the way He chooses.*

Psalm 25:12

Goal

To help each family member understand the characteristics of God.

Prayer Focus

Thank God for His character. Think of ways God has displayed each day's characteristic to your family. Example: Unit 1 — All-Knowing: God knew us before we were born, and knows how long we will live (Ps. 139:16).

▶ Who is God? How could He know the exact path for every one of the billions of people who have lived or will live on the earth? These basic questions about our awesome God will be answered in this week's lessons.

Unit 1

All-Knowing

One of the words that describes God is the word "omniscient." This is a theological term that refers to God's perfect knowledge and wisdom, His power to know all things.

God knows our thoughts from afar. He is acquainted with all our ways, knowing our words before they are on our tongues. Remember, we read that He knew us even before we were born:

> *For there is not a word on my tongue, but behold, O Lord, you know it altogether (Ps. 139:4).*

This means He knows everything, every single thing. He planned the details of every object He created so His universe would be just the way He wanted it to be.

As an example, when He was planning the sun, He had to create it to be an object that would burn for thousands upon thousands of ages. It would never grow cold or dim. It would give light and warmth to the planet He would create for His people — the planet earth.

He set our planet "twirling," to create a time when it would turn toward the sun for light and activity, and a time of darkness for our rest. He thought about everything He made, and at the perfect moment He spoke, saying, "Let there be...!" No sooner had He spoken those few words than *boom!* There it was!

Think about the beautiful birds He has given us to enjoy. Before He created a single bird, He thought about what it would eat and where it would nest. He made bushes and trees before He made birds. He planned their body structures and feathers so they could fly.

The book of Matthew tells us: "Look at the birds of the air, for they neither sow nor reap nor gather into barns; yet your heavenly Father feeds them. Are ye not of more value than they?" (6:26, KJV).

If God cares so much for the birds, does He not care much more for us? Because He knows everything, He knows what is best for us. And if we ask His help, He will direct our way!

DISCUSSION QUESTIONS

What do you think were some of the things God thought about before He created man?

Why should it make us happy to realize that God is "all-knowing"?

What are some of the decisions about our lives for which we should ask God's direction?

Describe one incident in which you felt God showed you a better way to do something than what you had planned to do.

Unit 2

All-Powerful

Children's Prayer Focus

Thank God for being here and ask Him to help you live for Him.

Another theological term used to describe God is the word "omnipotent." That word means there is nothing He cannot do. He is all-powerful.

Hebrews 1:3 says, "He upholds all things by the word of His power."

Do you remember when you were learning to ride a bicycle? There were times when you would get on that bike and pedal down the street while someone ran beside you helping you to balance the bike. You were not expected to start balancing on two wheels without help.

When we are learning to cook, someone needs to stay near, giving the help needed to make the food turn out right. When a driving instructor teaches a young person to drive a car, the instructor stays in the car, using dual controls to guard the student's feet and hands, making sure no accident occurs.

God is just like that. He does not leave us powerless to fight the temptations of the devil by ourselves. Nor does He say, "Keep my rules," and then stand back and laugh at us as we struggle to do right but fail. His power supports us. His strength teaches us to live the Christian life. His omnipotent power is ours to use. We only have to ask for it when we need it.

We can count on His power. It will never let us down.

▦ The Hayford Heritage ▦

Learning to like many foods — or being pleasant in the event we don't like something — is sometimes a difficult lesson. Our kids were required to have at least one spoonful of everything on the table, without a complaint or comment. Our two-and-a-half-year-old did not like squash, but *well* understood the rule. As Daddy lifted him into his chair, he eyed the table and mumbled distastefully, "Ugh, squash!"

Daddy quickly turned him about and asked, "What did you say?"

With an angelic smile and a complete change of tone, he repeated: "Mmm, squash!" (The old nature surfaces early.)

DISCUSSION QUESTIONS

Can you share an illustration from your life when you relied upon someone else to help you do something too hard for you to do alone?

What are some of the things that God is still teaching you?

What example can you give that shows how God's power helped you when you needed it the most?

In what area of your life do you need God's power to help you right now?

▶ *Parent Tip*

I am aware of the special needs and time limitations in single-parent homes. If you are a single parent, this time of sharing the Word with your children will create stability and security for children who have suffered the pain of losing a parent to death or divorce. You will reap a rich reward for your determined effort, even though it requires real planning and sacrifice on your part.

Unit 3

Creator

Before there was anything — even one little speck of sand — God *was!* When we try to imagine that, we can't. There was no sky, no land, no sea, no stars, no moon and no sun. It was as though the whole universe was one big empty room, and only God was there.

Then, in the beginning, God created the heavens and the earth.

God planned planet earth for a very special reason — to create a home for His most magnificent creation: people! When He had everything ready, He said, "Let Us make man in Our image" (Gen. 1:26). That is what makes us magnificent.

We would be brought forth in a different way than all other created things. God took some of the earth itself and molded Adam, the first person. Let's stop to think about that. If you or I were to take clay and try to shape a human body that looked perfect, we would only have a statue of man. Our statue would have no heart, stomach or lungs. It would not have real eyes to see with or a real nose to breathe with.

But God thought of everything that man would need to live. A brain with which to think and learn; bones, tendons and muscles to help him move; and blood to carry life throughout his body. When Adam had been perfectly formed, God knelt over Adam's lifeless figure and breathed His own breath into Adam, and man began to live.

God placed "seed" within everything He created so that each living thing could reproduce itself. Every bush, plant, tree and animal — from the tiniest bug to the greatest mammal — received this awesome gift of reproductive life. And man did too! Each created thing continues to bring forth its own kind, filling God's lovely world.

As Christians, when we look closely at our planet's wondrous creation, we do not doubt that it was made by our omniscient, omnipotent Creator-God. But many people in the world have been deceived into believing that it all just happened. Tomorrow we will take a closer look at some of the beliefs behind evolution, and discover that even modern science points to our Creator-God.

The psalmist recognized the work of creation and said:

By the word of the Lord the heavens were made, and all the host of them by the breath of his mouth...Let all the earth fear the Lord, let all the inhabitants of the world stand in awe of him. For he spoke, and it was done; he commanded, and it stood fast (Ps. 33:6,8-9).

DISCUSSION QUESTIONS

Ask the children to ask any questions they have about creation — or today's lesson. If there is anything you cannot answer with certainty, tell them you will look it up and share the answer tomorrow.

Ask things like: Why did God make bushes and trees before He made birds and animals?

Unit 4

An Awesome Designer*

We can see God's beautiful handiwork and design in the world around us.

Imagine an ordinary-looking beetle as it walks in front of a hungry frog. It looks like meal time for the frog, doesn't it? But a bombardier beetle points its two "cannons" and fires noxious gasses at 100°C into the frog's face.

A bombardier beetle has two specially designed chambers and two specially designed cannons. When gasses are forced out of the chambers and into the cannons, they mix and cause an explosion.

All the parts of the bombardier beetle must be working together at the same time. They couldn't have evolved by time and chance. The beetle was created by a Designer who had a plan and purpose

---

* This unit was contributed by Bill Gosselin, a high school science teacher at Calvary Assembly School, Winter Park, Florida.

— and great creativity!

How about the voracious barracuda floating at the bottom of the sea? Suddenly a tiny fish swims straight into the barracuda's mouth. But to the surprise of everyone, the barracuda does not eat the tiny visitor. It is a cleaner-fish, designed to eat parasites and food remains in the barracuda's mouth.

The creative genius of God designed an unusual team that works together. Instead of being enemies, both the barracuda and the cleaner-fish benefit from the relationship.

The sea anemone survives by eating fish it grabs and stings with its tentacles. But a specially designed clown fish is protected from the sting of the anemone by a protective layer on its scales. While it rests in the tentacles of the anemone, it is safe from bigger fish who might enjoy a "clown fish dinner" but who will not go near the deadly anemone.

Only a Creator could have made such a special combination. Our world is full of examples of God's wonderful handiwork. We only need to open our eyes and look around us.

> *For by Him all things were created that are in heaven and that are on earth, visible and invisible, whether thrones or dominions or principalities or powers. All things were created through Him and for Him (Col. 1:16).*

Yet today many people still deny the existence of a Master Designer, choosing to believe the theory of evolution. But there are many discrepancies in that theory.

If evolution were true, we should find hundreds of fossils showing the process of change from one organism into another. For example, we should find fossils of half-reptile/half-bird creatures. Or fossils of half-ape/half-man skeletons. These fossils would be called "transitional fossils." Charles Darwin, the father of evolution, admitted that the fossil record created was a big problem for his theory. He thought it would take about twenty years to find enough transitional fossils to prove evolution. It has been over 120 years since Darwin made that statement, and we still haven't found any.

All the fossils that have been collected show one fully developed organism. There are none showing half-reptile/half-bird creatures. And there are certainly none that reveal a half-ape/half-man creature.

God has given us marvelous evidence in the fossil record to support creation. God has not left the creationist standing alone. Our glorious Father has given more than enough scientific evidence to support creation. He is truly a Master Designer.

Unit 5

The One Who Lets Me Choose

Children's Prayer Focus

Thank God for allowing us to be part of His "forever family."

The Bible tells us "God is love" (1 John 4:8). Love is not always easy to explain. Love is not something you can see or touch, but we certainly can feel it, can't we?

People want to do things for the people they love. Parents love their families and work hard to provide a good home for them. Kids do nice things to show Mom and Dad how much they love them.

God created our planet for us, because He loves us. But the greatest evidence of His love existed even before He created our world. He had something else to share with man — eternity! His Word tells us that one day He will come and take us with Him to heaven, "And so shall we ever be with the Lord" (1 Thess. 4:17, KJV). It will be exciting to discover what heaven is really like!

Our bodies will die. They grow old and tired

and wear out. But because God breathed His life into man, the real person, the "me" who lives in this body, cannot die. Whether I live in heaven or hell, I will live forever. So, I surely want to be forgiven and cleansed of my sin! That is where Jesus comes into the picture.

Because God gave us a free will, you and I have been given the responsibility of making decisions for ourselves. If we are going to share eternity with God, we must choose God's Son and serve Him as the Lord of our life, choosing and doing His will. He will never force us to be good, but He wants us to choose to be good. If we have given our hearts to Him, His Spirit convicts our hearts of wrong actions.

Because God is very anxious for us to be with Him, He made a way for us to be forgiven. If we choose to have Jesus Christ live in our hearts, He will make our hearts clean and new. He loves every single one of us. He wants us to know Him, just as we know one another in our family, and become a part of God's "forever family."

DISCUSSION QUESTIONS

What are some of the things God created that you enjoy most of all?

What special gift did God give us that is even greater than earth?

How do our choices determine whether we will spend eternity with God?

What are some of the bad choices you have made in the past?

▶ *Parent Tip*

Today's lesson gives you a wonderful opportunity to be sure each family member has accepted Jesus Christ as his or her personal Savior. Talk about God's gift of salvation, then discuss this with your children individually at bedtime.

Encourage family members to think carefully about whether they have accepted Christ. If they indicate that they have, ask them to tell you when and how it happened.

Week 4

God's Forever Family

Goal

To grasp the truths about salvation and eternity for God's forever family.

Prayer Focus

Thank Jesus for preparing a home for us in heaven, mentioning that you know heaven has been prepared for all who receive Jesus as their Savior.

▶ As each child participates in the discussion times, select something they say and comment upon it favorably. Ask leading questions to aid younger children in the thinking process. Make a positive response to each contribution.

Unit 1

A Plan Before Time

When God created us with the ability to choose, He knew we would sometimes make wrong choices.

Before we even had life to lose, God loved us enough to save it! He prepared a way for us to be forgiven for our wrong choices.

Thousands of years would pass from the time God prepared the plan to the time when Jesus came to earth to live his life perfectly, overcoming every effort Satan made to try to destroy God's plan. But as you know, it was in God's plan for Jesus to win the battle against Satan. (How foolish of the devil to think he could defeat the Son of God.)

Now anyone who chooses to come to God and confess his or her sin can be forgiven — totally! God doesn't simply excuse our sinfulness. He is a holy God — and sin is very costly. It costs life. Jesus paid for man's sin so man could live with Him forever by making that one, important, *right* choice — asking Him to be our Savior.

Jesus speaks of Himself as our Shepherd. He wants to lead us and care for us, just as a shepherd cares for the sheep. He calls us His sheep, and says, "My sheep hear My voice, and I know them, and they follow Me. And I give them eternal life, and they shall never perish; neither shall anyone snatch them out of My hand" (John 10:27-28).

Choose to have Jesus in your life. Love Him for saving you. Build a wonderful friendship with Him. Talk to Him every day about your temptations and trials. Listen to what He says to you — it will help you to become wise and strong against Satan.

Remember that even before there was an earth, there was a plan of forgiveness. God said, "When I create man in My image, I will make a way for him to be with Me forever — if he chooses to accept My plan and serve Me."

Did you know that in His wonderful knowledge God has known since the beginning how you would choose? God's knowledge is mind-boggling.

DISCUSSION QUESTIONS

When did God know we would need a Savior?

What did sin cost?

What kind of choice does God want man to make?

As our Good Shepherd, how does God want to help us withstand the attacks of Satan?

Can you describe a time when God gave you the strength to overcome a temptation?

Unit 2

God Plays Only By the Rules

Children's Prayer Focus

Ask God to help us be truly sorry for our wrong choices.

Even though we have come to know God as very loving and very concerned about His people, we must understand that He has definite rules about everything. Let's take a look at some of His rules.

First, there is no other way to find forgiveness except through God's plan of salvation. Jesus said, "I am the way, the truth, and the life. No one comes to the Father except through Me" (John 14:6).

Second, we must choose repentance — it is our decision. To repent means "to turn and go the other way." We must confess any wrong that we know is in our hearts; then we must turn around and go the other way. God's way is the only right way for us to walk.

Third, we must have genuine sorrow for our

wrong-doing. We may do the same wrong thing over and over again. But our loving God does not judge us by what we have done wrong — He looks at our hearts. He is interested in how we feel about what we have done. "For the Lord does not see as man sees; for man looks at the outward appearance, but the Lord looks at the heart" (1 Sam. 16:7).

We have the Holy Spirit to convict us of sin. If God sees that we are genuinely sorry about our mistake or our act of disobedience, He will hear us when we repent. We must tell Him we are sorry and ask Him to make us strong. Then we must turn away from our sin.

God is very serious about sin. Although He will forgive us over and over again, without true repentance He will not even hear our prayers for forgiveness. We must have genuine sorrow in our hearts for missing the mark.

God teaches us that we must follow His example by learning to forgive others just as He forgives us. When Peter asked Jesus how many times he must forgive his brother, Jesus told him to forgive 490 times (Matt. 18:22). Jesus knew Peter would not be able to keep track of that many offenses.

Anyone who is walking in God's ways must follow His example in forgiveness. That means I must have a forgiving nature if I expect God to forgive me. (▶ Have each child comment on this.)

DISCUSSION QUESTIONS

What does repentance mean?

Does God expect you to be perfect and never sin? Then what does He expect from you?

How must I be like God in my actions toward other people?

Can you think of an illustration of a time when you needed to forgive someone over and over?

Unit 3

*New Life
In Christ*

It is such a blessing to receive Jesus as a child!
Just as an artist takes a lump of clay and fashions
it into a beautiful sculpture, God will take your life
and shape it into the beautiful design He planned
just for you.

It is very important that we learn to listen and
respond to the things that God speaks to us about.
He wants to develop in us the gifts and abilities
that will help us serve Him best with our lives.

It is also important for us to get to know God
through His Word. Jesus said, "I am the way, the
truth and the life" (John 14:5). Just as we follow a
map to show us how to reach our destination, God
has given us a sure way down the path of life to
arrive at our eternal destination — heaven. His
Word tells us what things we should do and those
we should avoid to make a safe journey to the

home He has prepared for us.

God's Word will make us wise in our spiritual lives. The apostle Paul commended his young friend, Timothy, because "from childhood you have known the Holy Scriptures, which are able to make you wise for salvation through faith which is in Christ Jesus" (2 Tim. 3:15).

Paul continued by reminding Timothy of the reason he should study God's Word. "All Scripture is given by inspiration of God, and is profitable for doctrine, for reproof, for correction, for instruction in righteousness, that the man of God may be complete, thoroughly equipped for every good work" (2 Tim. 3:16).

David understood the importance of God's Word. He wrote the longest chapter in the Bible to help us recognize how important God's Word is to our spiritual growth. In this chapter, he gave his personal opinion about God's Word when he stated, "Thy Word have I hid [memorized and understood] in my heart that I might not sin against Thee" (Ps. 119:11, KJV).

Getting to know God's written Word — the Bible — and God's living Word — Jesus Christ — is the best preparation for life we can have.

Jesus Himself told us: "He who has My commandments and keeps them, it is he who loves Me. And he who loves Me will be loved by My Father, and I will love him and manifest Myself to him" (John 14:21). (This means "become his real friend.")

DISCUSSION QUESTIONS

What advantages are there to receiving Christ as our Savior while we are children?

Why is it important to listen and respond to the things God says to each of us?

Can you list the reasons Paul gave to Timothy for studying the Scriptures?

What is your favorite Scripture verse? Why do you like this verse so much?

Unit 4

God's
Home Base

Children's Prayer Focus

*Thank God for preparing a home
for each of us in heaven.*

There are over five hundred references to heaven in the Bible. We learned in an earlier lesson that God sets up a command post in our hearts. But heaven is His *home base!*

God said, "Heaven is My throne, and earth is My footstool" (Is. 66:1). It may seem a little odd to think of earth as a "footstool." A footstool is not one of the most noticeable pieces of furniture in a home, but it is one of the most frequently used.

But God does not live only in heaven. Moses asked, "Who is able to build Him a temple, since heaven and the heaven of heavens cannot contain Him?" (2 Chr. 2:6). God cannot be contained by a location. We learned earlier that He is omnipresent — everywhere present.

Heaven is the place to which Jesus returned when He left earth. And He gave us a very special promise that He would come again for those who have accepted Him into their own lives: "In My Father's house are many mansions...I go to prepare a place for you. And if I go and prepare a place for you, I will come again and receive you to Myself; that where I am, there you may be also" (John 14:2-3).

What an awesome opportunity. We can live forever with God in His own home.

God is such a loving and wonderful God. He longs for every person to come and be with Him. It is never too late to repent and give Him your heart.

Even though the Bible tells us a little bit about heaven, we still cannot possibly imagine just what it will be like. Nor can we fully comprehend the glory of being in God's presence forever. We can only anticipate what it will be like.

The writer of Hebrews tries to help us understand what entering heaven will be like. He says: "But you have come to Mount Zion and to the city of the living God, the heavenly Jerusalem, to an innumerable company of angels, to the general assembly and church of the firstborn, who are registered in heaven, to God the Judge of all, to the spirits of just men made perfect, to Jesus the Mediator of the new covenant" (Heb. 12:22-24).

(▶ Talk about each segment of this passage in terms your children can both grasp and be awed by.)

Nothing can truly prepare us for the glory of heaven. We must wait in anticipation, living our lives as God directs, "looking for that blessed hope and glorious appearing of our great God and Savior Jesus Christ" (Titus 2:13).

DISCUSSION QUESTIONS

Where has God established His home base?

Why did Jesus return to heaven? What is He doing for us in heaven?

What is the requirement we must meet in order to spend eternity in heaven?

What do you think heaven will look like?

Can you describe how you think God may look when we see Him in heaven?

Unit 5

*A Home
In the Sky*

God did not give us a very detailed picture of heaven. The book of Revelation speaks of streets of gold, walls inlaid with precious jewels and a crystal sea. But still we cannot really imagine what heaven will look like.

It was after the apostle John was supernaturally given a vision of heaven that he wrote the book of Revelation. He described heaven as being filled with gold, crystal and precious jewels. I believe it was by the inspiration of God that he painted such a picture — using the most costly, beautiful things we know about to describe the beauty of heaven.

Today there are people who have gone through near-death experiences who have had visions of heaven. They describe heaven as being filled with a great light coming from a glorious presence they believed was God.

We may never have such an experience. But one thing we know — God is light! "In Him was life, and the life was the light of men" (John 1:4). Heaven is illuminated by the glory of God.

As we live our lives in hope of our eternal home with God in heaven, we can help others prepare their lives for eternity in heaven. There are three important steps we must take to be prepared to possess our home in the sky.

1. We must transfer our citizenship from
   earth to heaven.

When someone leaves another country to become a citizen of the United States, that person must meet the requirements for citizenship. We must also meet the spiritual requirements for citizenship in heaven. Paul told the Christians at Philippi: "For our citizenship is in heaven, from which we also eagerly wait for the Savior, the Lord Jesus Christ" (Phil. 3:20). The requirement for citizenship is believing on the Lord Jesus Christ as our Savior. When we accept Him into our lives, our citizenship is transferred from earth to heaven.

2. We must serve Christ on earth as we
   wait for heaven.

Through the parable of the ten servants, Christ instructed us to "Do business till I come" (see Luke 19:11-27). God intends for us to fulfill His plan on earth. He wants us to tell others about His plan of salvation. He would be so happy if everyone would choose to spend eternity with Him in heaven.

3. He wants us to be ready to be taken up
   with Jesus when He comes.

As a child, our author's eldest son, Jack, became concerned about who would go to be with Jesus when He comes to get all of His people.

"How do we know who will be taken up with Him, Mamma?" he asked his mother one day.

The Lord gave her the answer she needed: "Everyone who is 'taken up' with him now, Jack," she answered.

If your heart thinks about Him and wants to please Him, your mind is "taken up" already — and you can be sure you will be too.

Heaven will be ours someday. Let's live our lives in preparation, spreading the news of this wonderful opportunity to be God's forever family.

Week 5

Talk About God

Memory Verse

You shall teach them diligently to your children, and shall talk of them when you sit in your house, when you walk by the way, when you lie down, and when you rise up.

Deuteronomy 6:7

Goal
To make talking about God a natural part of your family life.

▣ The Hayford Heritage ▣

My husband and I used the evening meal time for talking about the Bible and God with our children, and in their own versions they continued this practice with their children. I am filled with joy as I watch four generations of our family, including three children, nine grandchildren and sixteen great-grandchildren following the biblical principles we taught.

Unit 1

Live by God's Rules When You Sit

Our memory verse is very specific about God's plan for teaching children. Not only does it tell us to be diligent about our teaching, but it also tells us four specific times when we are to apply the Word of God to our children's lives.

And these words which I command you today...you shall teach...diligently...when you sit in your house (Deut. 6:6-7).

The first specific direction God gives to us is to talk about God's rules for living "when you sit in your house." The people of Moses' day had less need for making this happen, but establishing this relationship early and being in proper control of all the things to which kids are exposed does require creative diligence on the parents' part.

Getting a family to sit together at home must start early and be fun. That is exactly why it is so important to have a planned time on a daily basis to sit down together to learn God's principles. Starting in early childhood (God's primary time to lay a foundation of faith), children grow up accepting the validity of His claim on their lives and determined to introduce something similar to their children in times to come.

When we committed to be Deuteronomy 6:7 parents, we decided that meal time was the best time for us. (▶ I hope by now you have selected a consistent time to meet. This scheduled time should be a family priority. Talk with your children about your responsibility to God and your goals for them.)

Our family can have the same heritage of godliness that the Hayfords have had the joy of experiencing to the fourth generation. To keep the discussions challenging, we will change the format as you grow older. When you become parents, you may lead your family times with God differently than we do ours. But it will be a normal progression of spiritual growth in our family.

God's directive was: Teach when you "sit in your house." Here we are — sitting in our house together and learning!

DISCUSSION QUESTIONS

What is most enjoyable about our time together?

What one part of our devotions has been most helpful to you?

What would you like to do differently?

What do you imagine your family devotions will be like with your own children?

▶ *Parent Tip*

Talk to your children about the Great Commission. Then impress upon them that witnessing is useless if it is not lived as well as spoken. Pray that each life is so impressive it creates curiosity in unsaved friends. "Be ready always to give an answer to every man that asketh you a reason of the hope that is in you" (1 Pet. 3:15).

Unit 2

Walk By the Way

The second specific direction God gave to parents through Moses was to talk about His rules "when you walk by the way."

Back in the time when our memory verse was written, there were few other ways to get anywhere. Families walked to the places they wanted to go. Even if they were going to move from one town to another, they walked together. Today, any time we are moving from one place to another is a great time to talk with each other about the things that really matter. It could be going to or coming from school, going shopping or perhaps just walking around the block.

When we travel, we can watch for wonderful things God created that demonstrate His care for us.

Our family can discover what God wants to say to us about even the smallest things we see along the way. All of nature cries out "God did this!" Point out the regularity of the seasons and the subtle changes that indicate to us what is coming.

Tell them about the benefits that come from the farmer resting his land, even the forced rest that comes with the winter storms.

Suggest that everyone watch for something that is totally natural — nothing that man has done — and what the most interesting thing is about it.

Luanne Hayford always liked stones. At one time she had a small stone polisher. She remarked one day at the beach how God polished the stones so long they became sand. But He made the seashells out of "harder stuff" so the pattern would stay on them.

Kids have these remarkably interesting things to share if we give them time. Perhaps they are not too scientifically correct, but who cares?

When you are traveling, it is a good time to talk about the things you have been learning as a family. It is a great time to play games.

Have special secrets with each child: "What is your dream, or hope, that you haven't ever told anyone? Maybe it is something we can help you realize." (Both parents should be "in" on the secret, but it should be honored.) Each child should know that all the others have secrets too.

▶ *Parent Tip*

Plan for lively discussions. Commend each child for his or her specific contributions. We are depositing into our children's hearts a sense of awe about our value to God. Our goal is to "love Him because He first loved us."

Unit 3

When You Lie
Down — Pray

Children's Prayer Focus

*Pray for a sense of God's presence as
we go to bed each night.*

Our memory verse says, "And these words...you
shall teach...diligently to your children...when you lie
down" (vv. 6-7).

What do we do at bedtime every night? God
knows that taking the time to talk about Him at the
end of the day will help each family member rest
better. We can thank Him for all the good things
that happened and tell Him we are sorry for anything we did that was wrong. He forgives us and
gives us a nice clean heart.

Bedtime is also a wonderful time to talk with
each other about the things that are troubling us
and to straighten out any problems. God's Word
advises us, "Do not let the sun go down on your
wrath" (Eph. 4:26).

God knows that we need to have our minds free
of problems so we can rest well and have pleasant

dreams. Children need a reasonably early bedtime. That is why we have set a bedtime for you. When parents do not get enough rest, the stresses and frustrations that they face during the day make life difficult.

A good night's rest is the best preparation for all of us to expect tomorrow to be a good day. Each day is filled with opportunities for learning and growing. We don't want to waste these opportunities by being too tired to learn. We want our minds to be sharp and alert.

Falling asleep each night thinking about Jesus is one of the most wonderful habits we can cultivate. Bedtime becomes a time when our minds have nothing more to do except think about Jesus. The following verses give us three special "bedtime thoughts" for these special moments of spiritual reflection.

1. It is God Himself who gives us a good night's rest:

    I will both lie down in peace, and sleep; for You alone, O Lord, make me dwell in safety (Ps. 4:8).

2. God, who never sleeps, can speak to us even while we sleep:

    For God may speak...in a dream, in a vision of the night, when deep sleep falls upon men. Then He opens the ears of men, and seals their instruction (Job 33:14-16).

3. God will prove His faithfulness and mercy anew to us each morning:

    Through the Lord's mercies we are not consumed, because His compassions fail not. They are new every morning; great is Your faithfulness (Lam. 3:22-23).

Falling asleep each night thinking about God and His love and mercy toward us, and waking each morning in anticipation of what He will do to guide and protect us that day, is the best insurance for happiness of heart.

▶ *Parent Tip*

Bedtime is one of the times when a child is likely to share troubling thoughts. This special time should be planned and not rushed. Your kids will enjoy the personal attention you give them individually at bedtime. Spend time with each child, rotating from night to night. Pray together about the unique needs and concerns of each child.

Unit 4

When You
Rise Up — Obey

Children's Prayer Focus

*Pray for happy, relaxed mornings
together as a family.*

Our memory verse concludes: "Talk about them...when you rise up" (v. 7).

Parental attitude in the morning sets the mood for the entire family. Many times, chaos reigns supreme because of poor planning. Talking to each other, let alone talking about God, is almost impossible.

But God has a much different perspective on mornings. The psalmist gives us an example of how God wants us to feel about the morning.

> *My voice You shall hear in the morning,*
> *O Lord; in the morning I will direct it to*
> *You, and I will look up (Ps. 5:3).*

Getting the day off to a happy start takes organization. Preparation for the morning should begin the night before. Homework should be completed and school clothes laid out ready for morning. Plan your schedule so the family can have breakfast together to give everyone a good beginning for the day. This means everyone is to be at the table on time, ready for the day.

It took a conscious effort of the will for the psalmist to direct his voice to God in the morning. How can we focus our attention on God as we start our day?

The psalmist goes on to tell us:

> *Cause me to hear your lovingkindness in the morning; for in you do I trust; cause me to know the way in which I should walk, for I lift my soul up to You (Ps. 143:8).*

In this verse the psalmist was ready to trust God for this day, to ask Him to direct his steps for what lay ahead in the next twenty-four hours. What a change this attitude would have on the way we live each day. It would give us a victorious attitude. We would be able to exclaim with the psalmist:

> *This is the day the Lord has made; we will rejoice and be glad in it (Ps. 118:24).*

Attitude is a matter of our will. God wants us to begin our day with confidence and joy! Let's "get God into the day" before "the day gets into the family."

DISCUSSION QUESTIONS

What hinders you from being good-natured in the morning?

How can we acknowledge the lordship of Jesus in the morning?

What can you do to help us "get God into our day"?

▶ *Parent Tip*

Praise music, preferably without lyrics, played softly enough to create atmosphere is a nice way to awaken the household. It "soothes the savage beast" that wants to stay in bed and doze. Having order in your home is valuable emotional security for everyone. If this is a major change, let it be understood that it is a necessary change, and you will expect full cooperation.

Unit 5

First-Time Obedience

Throughout all your life you will be subject to people who have authority over you. Teachers, bosses, policemen — all of these are a part of life.

In order to receive God's approval, parents must teach their children to live by God's rules. Right now, while you are living in a family that loves you and understands your mistakes as you learn, is the best time to learn God's rules.

His rules not only teach us *what* to do but also *why* it is important to do it. We are to respond in a pleasing manner. When a parent calls a child, the response should not be "Huh?" or "What do you want?" The child should not yell, "Just a minute!"

We are going to begin working on first-time obedience. When I call you, I will say your name and then quickly add, "Remember?" That will remind you not to say anything until you come to me face-to-face and say, "Yes, Mom (or Dad)?"

Then I will tell you the reason I called and ask if you understand what I told you to do.

I do not call you unless it is important to talk with you about something. Sometimes *now* is the only time a thing can be taken care of. A pleasant response is God's way to respond to anyone who has authority over you — whether it's a parent, a teacher, a baby sitter or an older adult.

Christ is our example of obedience. The New Testament contrasts His obedience with the disobedience of Adam (see Romans 5). Christ's obedience is referred to as a "gift" (Rom. 5:15). By His gift of obedience we have salvation and eternal life.

A child's immediate, pleasant response to a parent's command is also a "gift." It brings joy and love into that moment. A child's disobedience creates unpleasantness for everyone.

God wants children to obey with happy and willing hearts. Together we can find pleasant ways to take care of everything.

Remember:

Hear instruction and be wise, and do not disdain it (Prov. 8:33).

DISCUSSION QUESTIONS

What is "first-time obedience"?

Can you describe a time when it was hard for you to obey quickly?

What are some of the feelings you have when you choose to be disobedient and not respond quickly when you are called?

What one word describes how you feel when you obey immediately?

▶ *Parent Tip*

Ask each child to think of something for which he or she is most frequently disciplined, something he or she would like to try to improve this week. Ask each child to report in each day on how he or she is improving in this area. Pray daily about these improvements, praising the children for their successes and encouraging their obedience.

Week 6

*Learning the Joy
of Obedience*

Memory Verse

*Children, obey your parents in all things,
for this is well pleasing to the Lord.*

Colossians 3:20

Goal

To establish an environment of obedience within
your home.

Prayer Focus

As each session begins, pray for God's presence
and help in understanding (Ps. 25:12). Ask the
Holy Spirit to seal His Word in your children's
hearts (John 14:26).

▶ Kids who learn to express their understanding of
Scripture in an accepting family setting become
bolder about expressing themselves in all situations, especially in oral academic involvement.
They become more confident in Bible truths.

Unit 1

The Rewards
Of Obedience

God gave us rules to teach us to make right choices. Many people (even some Christians) believe that we no longer need the Ten Commandments, because we are not "under law, but under grace" (Rom. 6:14). We must remember that God's Word says: "All Scripture is given by inspiration of God, and is profitable for doctrine, for reproof, for correction, for instruction in righteousness" (2 Tim. 3:16).

Today we are beginning several weeks of study about God's rules. They will help our lives to run smoothly and they will bring rewards to our lives.

Our world situation today is a result of these laws being set aside. The results of these acts of disobedience affect every person in our world. A world filled with people who make their own rules is a world out of control.

The Bible helps us to discover the rewards of obedience. Today we will examine four of these rewards. (▶Allow family members to read the following Scriptures. Ask the reader to identify the reward of obedience mentioned in each verse.)

1. Prosperity and pleasure in life (Ps. 37:25).
2. The power of the Holy Spirit in our lives (Acts 5:32).
3. Release from the oppression of enemies (Ex. 23:22).
4. To become a "special treasure" to God (Ex. 19:5-6).

▶ *Parent Tip*

You will need to lead your children to see unique ways each of these rewards can apply to your family. For example: By obeying God's rule to "love your enemies," it may be possible to turn the kid who is bullying you daily at school into one of your friends — thus being released from his oppression. Or, by honoring your parent's request to put your allowance in a savings account instead of buying lots of candy, you can save enough to get the CD player you want — thus enjoying the prosperity and pleasures of life.

DISCUSSION QUESTIONS

In what ways has God prospered our family and brought it pleasures?

How has the power of the Holy Spirit been helpful in your life?

What does Exodus 23:22 tell us God will do for us if we obey His instructions to us?

How has God helped you to know that you are His special treasure?

▶ Read Malachi 3:16. Ask the children: "Is this what we are doing? Are we precious to God?"

Unit 2

Why We Have House Rules

Children's Prayer Focus

*Ask God to help you
choose to obey.*

We will be taking a close look at God's rules — the Ten Commandments — in some later lessons.

Every business, school, office and club has rules that must be followed. Even street gangs and cults demand that its members follow the rules.

Our home has house rules, also. Can you name some of our house rules?

The house rules that we have established here at our home regard things that all of us should (or should not) do to make our home the very best place to live. I want to help you understand these rules. You should know why certain things are required of each of you. These rules are for everyone's good.

Why is it necessary to have rules? What happens when we disobey the rules? What happens when we obey?

(▶ This might take several days.) Begin today to read the twenty-seventh and twenty-eighth chapters of Deuteronomy to your kids. Stop to explain the meanings, but emphasize God's desire to provide and care for us.

Afterward, point out that disobedience produces a lot of misery — not because God is mad at us, but because He cannot bless disobedience.

Our house rules work in the same way. There are blessings for obeying the rules, and there are disciplines for being disobedient. But the choice is yours — do you want to be blessed or cursed?

Did you notice how our memory verse ends? It lets you see that God cares how you behave. He is pleased when He sees your obedience. Children feel wonderful when a parent smiles, compliments their behavior and says, "I'm so proud of you!" God wants to smile at you, too. He is well-pleased with kids who mind their parents!

DISCUSSION QUESTIONS

Why is it necessary for a family to establish rules within the home?

Can you think of a time when you received a blessing by being obedient?

Think of a time when you were disobedient. What discipline did you choose by your disobedience?

How do you really feel about having rules to obey?

Unit 3

The Devil Wants Me to Disobey

Who causes the trouble we fall into when we break the laws God has given us? (▶ Children will frequently answer this question by saying, "The devil does it!")

The devil, our enemy, *does* tempt us and endeavor to seduce us into wrongdoing. But neither God nor the devil is responsible for the end result — that is our own doing. We decide to do wrong. We choose to disobey God's rules.

The devil rejoices, and God sorrows. The devil knows it will be easier to get us to do wrong the second time around! God's sorrow is *for* us, not *because of* us. He is well aware of the burden of guilt when we have taken a "wrong turn" deliberately. God knows that once we have weakened and made a bad choice, the devil will try to take us farther away from God than we are already.

The devil (who is the god of this world) knows that his time is very short. When Jesus comes back and establishes His kingdom on earth, it will be all over for Satan. He knows that it saddens God's heart when he tricks one of us. That is his main goal — to grieve the heart of God!

▶ *Parent Tip*

Teach your children to resist the attempts of Satan to get them to make wrong choices. Encourage them to use their "spiritual armor" to withstand his attacks. Memorize the following verses:

> *Put on the whole armor of God, that you may be able to withstand in the evil day, and having done all, to stand. Stand therefore, having girded your waist with truth, having put on the breastplate of righteousness, and having shod your feet with the preparation of the gospel of peace;*
>
> *Above all, taking the shield of faith with which you will be able to quench all the fiery darts of the wicked one. And take the helmet of salvation, and the sword of the Spirit, which is the word of God;*
>
> *Praying always with all prayer and supplication in the Spirit (Eph. 6:13-18).*

DISCUSSION QUESTIONS

Why is the statement "the devil made me do it" an untrue statement?

What are some of the ways the devil tempts us to do wrong?

What do you think is the most important thing to know about the devil?

In what areas of your life do you find it hardest to resist the devil's temptations?

What is Satan's main goal?

▣ The Hayford Heritage ▣

Luanne once shared this thought with us: "Every day is election day. God votes for you to be obedient, Satan votes for you to be disobedient — and you cast the deciding vote."

Unit 4

Who's The Boss?

A parent would not allow a twelve-year-old boy to leave home and live in an apartment by himself. A twelve-year-old is not yet able to be completely responsible for his own actions. He doesn't even know all the rules yet.

Just when is a person capable of running his own life successfully? Much depends upon the circumstances in which the person was raised.

Teaching God's laws as fool-proof guides rather than "no-nos" (or "do-its") — then making those laws family practice — is your part, parent.

Children raised in the "nurture and admonition of the Lord" have the best chance of maturing early. Having witnessed in their home that God's laws are the "word," they are more likely to choose to live by those rules. Some teens who have been properly trained manage their own lives remarkably well.

Choice, of course, is the pivotal point, and how you as the parent deal with wrong choices in the formative years is going to play an important part in the finished product. Failing to discipline a child creates a person who will not discipline himself.

The chain of authority for our home begins with God — all of us must obey Him. Next, God has given parents authority over each child. We are to train you to choose honesty, morality and civility. We are to acquaint you with God, and why it is actually His love for the human family that requires us to adopt these principles. They will prepare you for situations you will face later when you are on your own — perhaps at college or even in your own home — and faced with making important decisions.

We must obey the rules of a city as long as we are located within the city boundaries. Our authorities are the governmental officials who have been elected to lead the city government. When you are within the boundaries of your school, you must respect the principal, the teachers and the regulations in that school.

God has established lines of spiritual authority as well. Those lines begin with God, move down to the pastors of a church, to the church officials, to the teachers and finally reach the congregation.

Those who have spiritual authority teach us God's rules. They remind us of the results of obedience or disobedience by teaching us from God's

Word. They help us make right choices and teach us that we have power to overcome when we are tempted to make wrong choices.

God's rules are very important today, just as they were for the Israelites who followed Moses.

DISCUSSION QUESTIONS

Why did God establish boundaries and authorities for us to follow?

Why must we learn to be responsible for our own actions?

Can you give an example of a time when you were protected from danger by obeying an authority over you?

Can you tell about a time when accepting responsibility for a wrong action brought discipline to you?

Unit 5

Courtesy to Mom and Dad

Children's Prayer Focus

Pray for God to help you show courtesy to your parents.

Obedience to a parent includes being courteous. If I called you when you were playing a game, what might you do? What do you think would happen if you came to me and said courteously, "Do you want me for something I could do in a little while? It's almost my turn, and I don't want to miss my turn!" What do you think I would say? (▶ Get responses.)

Most of the time I would be willing to wait for you to take your turn, but there will be times when I need you "right this minute"! At those times I might answer: "Honey, I am really sorry, but I *do* need you right now! I have garbage to throw away, and the trash can in the kitchen is overflowing. Since it is your responsibility to empty it, I need you to come right now and take the garbage out to the trash can in the garage and put a new garbage bag in the kitchen trash can. It won't take very long, and then you can get back to your game."

Would it show God's kind of obedience if you responded nicely? How should I respond if you are grumpy? (▶ Get responses.) I know how difficult it is to have to leave something that's really fun, but we are a family, and we work together as a team.

What are some ways to show team spirit to your parents? How can you show courtesy? Honor your parents? (▶ Get responses from the kids first, then offer suggestions.) How about:

- volunteering to do a chore?
- bringing in the groceries?
- not interrupting a conversation or phone call?
- being quiet when your parents are resting?
- speaking to your parents when you come in from outside?
- thanking your mother for a good meal?
- thanking your dad for driving you to your ballgame?

Happy obedience is the most important thing you can give to us, your parents. It is the way you help to make our home what God wants it to be.

Honoring us with little, helpful surprises is far more precious to us than any gift you could buy.

▨ The Hayford Heritage ▨

We used to select well-known children's Bible stories from each segment of Scripture and developed creative ways to relate each story. The children retold the story until they had it down *pat.* Then we pointed out the two-fold reason it was in the Bible: 1) to show us how God's rules worked and 2) to discover how the story affected our family.

Stories children love from God's Word:

Law — Abraham, the flood, the escape from Egypt.

History — Joshua's long day, Esther, Samson, Samuel, David and Solomon.

Major Prophets — Daniel, Jeremiah.

Minor Prophets — tithing (Malachi), our preciousness to God.

Gospels — Jesus' life: birth, flight to Egypt, ministry years, last week, crucifixion, resurrection.

Acts — Jesus' return to heaven, Paul's conversion, Stephen's martyrdom, Dorcas, the boy who fell out the window.

Epistles — a wide variety of stories about Christian living.

Revelation — heaven, condition of the lost.

Expand your children's knowledge of God's Word.

Thirty-Seven Words That Say It All

1. PUT GOD FIRST.

2. MAKE NO SUBSTITUTES.

3. HONOR GOD'S NAME.

4. KEEP HIS DAY.

5. RESPECT YOUR PARENTS.

6. DO NOT MURDER.

7. KEEP YOUR LOVE FOR ONE PARTNER.

8. DO NOT STEAL.

9. DO NOT LIE.

10. DO NOT WANT WHAT BELONGS TO OTHERS.

In these thirty-seven words, we see the heart of all God commanded His people — then and now. These are the Ten Commandments by which God wants us to live (see Deut. 5:6-22).

Thirty-Seven Words That Say It All, a sermon by Jack Hayford (The Church on the Way, Van Nuys, California).

Put God First

Memory Verse

You shall love the Lord your God with all your heart, with all your soul, and with all your mind. This is the first and great commandment.

Matthew 22:37-38

Goal

To find ways to place God first in our hearts, attitudes and actions.

Prayer Focus

Ask God to help us understand that our hearts are selfish, and to understand how loving God's ways will help us change from day to day. Lay hands on each child and bless them each day this week.

Unit 1

Putting God First Because He Is

Children's Prayer Focus

Ask God to help us make Him number one in our hearts.

When we care more about what someone might think or say about us than what pleases God, we are putting *us* first. We are making ourselves *God,* because He is the one that should have first place.

Why does God want us to realize He is number one? Why does God have the "right" to be number one? Do words or actions show that your heart's desire is to put God first? (▶ Allow each family member to contribute to the discussion.)

The Ten Commandments are part of God's covenant with His people. A covenant is an agreement between two people. God promised that we would be "a special treasure" to Him if we kept His laws (Ex. 19:5). When the intent of our heart is to put God first, our outward actions will reveal it. It is God's plan to share what His character is like through the actions of His people.

Because God created us, He knows exactly what is best for us. He wants us to have a good life. Deep within our hearts — within the real us — He put our "conscience." It is like a smoke alarm; it lets us know if something is wrong. If we wonder — even just a little bit — if something is wrong, then we need to stop what we are doing and put God first. If we are not sure what our conscience is trying to tell us, we may pray and ask God, or we can ask our parents or a pastor or Sunday school teacher.

Sometimes we will hear someone say, "The Lord told me." God speaks to us in many ways, but usually He speaks to our conscience. Some people refer to this as "the still, small voice down deep inside." Rarely does God talk in a voice we can hear with our ears. But He speaks to us deep in our conscience, where we hear differently and truly.

Sometimes, when we are trying to decide if something is right or wrong, we feel sort of nervous or *scared* — "If I do this, I may get in trouble!" That is a good time to choose *not* to do that thing. God has many ways to help us choose to do right. If you do not feel happy, or at peace, within your heart, put God first and change your actions.

DISCUSSION QUESTIONS

Can you list some ways that you could show God He is "number one" in your life?

Can you name some people you really admire who have placed God first in their lives in a specific way?

Can you think of some things our family can do that would show others God is first?

In what ways have you heard God speaking to you?

Can you tell about one time when your conscience directed you to make a right choice?

Unit 2

Don't Cheat
On God

We all use the word "cheat," but can you tell me
what it means? The dictionary says it means "to
deprive of something valuable by the use of deceit
or fraud."

We must not cheat God. We are a valuable treasure
to God when we obey His rules. And we must not
deprive Him of this treasure — or deceive others —
by saying we are His but not doing things in His
way.

Maybe, while you are playing a game, one of
your teammates tells the others a way to cheat and
win the game. The right choice for you as a
Christian would be to say, "I don't believe in cheating." Putting God first when your friends may
laugh at you or get mad at you is hard.

Someone may say, "Oh, it's only a game. Are you
going to make us lose by being a poor sport?" Or

your best friend might call you "Miss Goody-Two-Shoes," or some other name to make fun of you.

Your peers can be very hurtful. You may be excluded from their social groups, made fun of and even physically attacked because you refuse to be "one of the gang."

That's really tough, isn't it? No one likes to be ridiculed. The devil uses this way to make God's people afraid to do the right thing. He tries to make God's way seem silly, hard and unfair.

It is good to stand up to this kind of talk. You don't have to find fault with people who do these things. Just say, "Cheating is really stealing. If we cheat now, the next time someone will probably cheat us. I'm not mad at any of you, but I'm not going to cheat." Then, if necessary, offer to get out of the game. Later someone may ask you to explain and you can be a witness to them.

It is better to have one or two good friends who share your values than to go the way of less honest kids in the hope of getting along with them.

DISCUSSION QUESTIONS

Have you ever cheated God from having first place in your actions? How? What happened? How did you feel?

My husband and I came to Christ during a time of great spiritual revival — and were privileged to be discipled by a pastor who made it very clear that the demoralized state of our nation was the result of a breakdown in obedience to God's rules for family living. He made it plain that children will not grow up to be spiritually strong if they are being raised by parents who are spiritually weak.

Above all else we might ever accomplish, we wanted our kids to grow up knowing God's Word and understanding that one of God's priorities is to give us abundant joy in our lives. His "do" and His "don't" are intended to bring us into that joy.

When we accepted Christ as our Savior, our eldest, Jack, was sixteen months of age. In the years following our conversion, we grew both in our spiritual discernment and in the size of our family.

We decided to take the evening meal time to discuss their Sunday school lessons and to familiarize them with God's Word.

Our kids not only learned the stories from God's Word, but from the stories they also learned to put God first in their lives.

Unit 3

What Is An Idol?

We are to have no other "gods" than God. There are people in every nation of the world, including ours, who worship other gods.

Through a portion of Scripture in the book of Isaiah, the Bible shows us the foolishness of trying to create an idol. Listen as I read:

> *[The craftsman] plants a pine, and the rain nourishes it. Then it shall be for a man to burn, for he will take some of it and warm himself; yes, he kindles it and bakes bread...*
>
> *He burns half of it in the fire; with this half he eats meat. He roasts a roast, and is satisfied....*
>
> *And the rest of it he makes into a god, his carved image. He falls down before it*

and worships it, prays to it and says,
"Deliver me, for you are my god!"

And no one considers in his heart, nor
is there knowledge nor understanding to
say, "I have burned half of it in the fire,
yes, I have also baked bread on its coals;
I have roasted meat and eaten of it; and
shall I make the rest of it an abomination?
Shall I fall down before a block of
wood?...A deceived heart has turned him
aside; and he cannot deliver his soul, nor
say, "Is there not a lie in my right hand?"
(Is. 44:14-20).

This story sounds ridiculous to us. It is telling us about a man who is a master woodcutter. He makes his living by planting, growing and cutting down trees. He know more about trees than the average person does.

One day this man cuts down a tree that he has watched grow from a small sapling. Part of the tree, probably the smaller branches and twigs, he uses as kindling wood in his fireplace. As the wood burns, he roasts some meat over it for his family's dinner meal.

Yet this same man takes part of the tree, perhaps a smooth piece of the trunk, and carves the wood into an idol. And suddenly this man, who planted the tree with his own hands, watched it grow and even cut it down, looks at the idol he carved himself and says, "Wow, this is God!" The Bible verses tell us that he even falls down on his face and worships that piece of wood.

Idols don't have to be made of wood. They can be many different things. If you desire above all else to have, or be like, some one or some thing, that person or thing becomes a modern-day idol. Can you name a few examples of this?

Anything or anybody that is more important to us than God is an idol. They can be houses, land, cars or even CDs. Objects of worship, or idols, may also include things like fame, reputation, hobbies, pride or even things we do in the name of the Lord.

Many of the things that become idols to people today are just like the woodcutter's tree. They are things that the people know are not really God — but they have become so important to them that they give these things more prominence in their lives than they do God Himself.

Idolatry is a dangerous and deceitful sin. An idol is anything that stands between us and God. It is something we substitute for God.

God's rule is very clear: "Make no substitutes!"

Unit 4

The Hidden Idols
Of the Heart

God knows that our hearts can possess hidden idols. The Bible says:

> *The heart is deceitful above all things,
> and desperately wicked; who can know it?
> I, the Lord, search the heart, I test the
> mind, Even to give every man according
> to his ways, according to the fruit of his
> doings (Jer. 17:9-10).*

When David sinned against the Lord by making his relationship with Bathsheba more important than obeying the Lord, he cried out to God by saying:

> *Create in me a clean heart, O God, and renew
> a steadfast spirit within me (Ps. 51:10).*

In the New Testament, Jesus tried to explain to the scribes and Pharisees that it is our hearts that defile us. He exposed some of the hidden idols of the heart when He said:

> *Are you also still without understanding? Do you not yet understand that whatever enters the mouth goes into the stomach and is eliminated? But those things which proceed out of the mouth come from the heart, and they defile a man. For out of the heart proceed evil thoughts, murders, adulteries, fornications, thefts, false witness, blasphemies. These are the things which defile a man (Matt. 15:16-20).*

We must guard our hearts to keep out the things that could defile us and separate us from God. Nothing except God is to have first place in our hearts. Even good things can take His place in our hearts. You must "Keep your heart with all diligence, for out of it spring the issues of life" (Prov. 4:23).

Our hearts were created to be filled with God. But He cannot come into a place that is already filled. Even little things, if they are hidden in our hearts, can keep Him from being first. Never let that happen. Anything we guard and keep secret is an idol.

DISCUSSION QUESTIONS

What actually is an idol?

Can you give an example of something we might make into an idol?

Is money a bad thing?

A nice home?

A special friend?

Unit 5

I Just Don't Have Time for God

Another way God is often displaced is by us being too busy for Him. Life today is much busier than it was in the time of Moses. Sitting down to talk with neighbors about God was easy when the only alternative was talking to sheep.

Many people in our own nation do not make time for God even though they are surrounded by churches. Life is crammed full of activity, and Americans have learned to do so many things. Our own skills often lead us into the sin of idolatry as we become too involved in our leisure pursuits.

Let us today make a commitment *not* to let this happen. When we began these discussions, we determined to set aside a time each day to focus on God. Now, weeks later, we have already seen how difficult it is at times to keep that commitment.

How has the time we've spent with God

changed the way you feel about something?

▩ The Hayford Heritage ▩

We had been telling the story of Elijah on Mount Carmel as he taunted the prophets of Baal by saying, "Maybe your god is asleep." Our four-year-old son, Jim, was listening intently and suddenly blurted out: "Jesus doesn't go to bed!"

My husband quickly responded, "That's right, Jim. How do you know that?"

"I don't know," Jim blandly replied.

"Did Daddy or Mamma tell you that?" his older sister, Luanne, asked.

"Nope," Jim answered.

"Jim, you're telling us something we need to remember," my husband continued. "What makes you know God doesn't go to bed?"

Thoughtfully (I believe the Holy Spirit gave him the words), Jim told us: "Well, we pray when we eat, and we pray at bedtime. And if I have a bad dream, you come and pray in the middle of the night and Jesus hears us — so that means He doesn't sleep." Then he fell back in his chair as if to say, "That was a lot of work!"

Because God was a normal part of our life "around the clock," Jim concluded that God was always paying attention to him!

DISCUSSION QUESTIONS

Spend time together today as a family thinking of some creative ways to study God's Word. This would be a good time to have a game night with the game plan on pages 187-189 of this book. Develop a plan for helping each family member become acquainted with the entire Bible (see page 116).

Week 8

Honor God's
Name and Day

Goal

To develop methods for honoring God's name and
for setting aside a day for worshipping God.

Prayer Focus

Focus on specific ways to honor God better. Pray
about some creative ways your family can make
Sunday a special day for worshipping God and
developing your family relationship.

▶ We shape our children's attitude toward Sunday,
the Lord's Sabbath day, by the things we do. You
do not need to be legalistic, but it would be a valuable project to work on — developing the spiritual
life of your family by what you do on God's day.

Unit 1

A Commandment
For God's People

The third commandment is probably familiar to you. It reads: "You shall not take the name of the Lord your God in vain, for the Lord will not hold him guiltless who takes His name in vain" (Ex. 20:7).

Unfortunately, hearing people disobey this commandment is all too familiar to us. It is almost impossible to watch a television program without this hearing profanity. Every day we go to school and work with people who think nothing of using the Lord's name in vain.

But today I want you to think about this one important fact: This commandment wasn't given to people who do not know God; it was given to God's people! We can expect to hear unsaved people use God's name in vain — they haven't made a commitment to follow God's rules. There is a saying that states: "You can't blame dogs for barking, because that is what dogs do. And you can't blame a sinner for sinning, because that is what they do!"

But God's people have committed themselves to follow God's rules. It is important that we understand this commandment as it applies to Christians.

Christians should not swear. Our mouths are meant to proclaim God's glory. In the book of Psalms we are taught the right use of His name:

> *I will sing praise to thy name (9:2).*

> *They that know thy name will put their trust in thee (9:10).*

> *In the name of our God we will set up our banners (20:5).* (▶ Explain)

> *Let us exalt his name together (34:3).*

> *Through thy name will we tread them under that rise up against us (44:5). (Who is "them"?)*

> *Thou hast given me the heritage of those that fear thy name (61:5). (What is the heritage?)*

> *His name shall endure for ever: his name shall be continued as long as the sun (72:17).*

Give unto the Lord the glory due unto his name (96:8).

Our help is in the name of the Lord, who made heaven and earth (124:8).

God's name is never to be treated lightly, without respect or in a dishonoring way. It is God's name that gives us victory over the enemy.

▣ The Hayford Heritage ▣

Jim was youngest, and was always involved with younger boys in our neighborhood. I remember well an occasion when he came home from college for a weekend. The neighbor boys were playing football out in the street in front of our house. As Jim pulled his car into our driveway, one of the boys called out gruffly: "OK, guys, no cussin'! Hayford's home, and he don't like it!"

Unit 2

Using God's Name For No Purpose

Children's Prayer Focus

Pray that your friends can see you are "for real" about God.

There is another way that we must take care not to break this rule about God's name. "In vain" can also mean "for no real purpose."

Small children love to play "dress up." A little three-year-old boy might pretend to be "just like Daddy," wearing his father's shoes and sport coat and carrying his father's briefcase as he tells his Mom, "I gotta go to work now." Or a girl is transformed into a famous movie actress by putting on her mother's fancy evening gown, high heels and make-up.

Dress-up is a wonderful make-believe activity for children. But playing dress-up with our Christianity is a way of using the Lord's name for no real purpose.

Some people call themselves Christians (and may even think that they are), but if they have not asked Jesus to be their Savior, they are not Christians. Other people *fake* Christianity. Maybe at one time they were living for the Lord. Now they no longer live for Him but try to hide the fact. Some young people struggle with trying to please both their unsaved friends and their Christian parents. When they are with their friends, they do whatever their friends do. But they behave differently when they come home so their parents won't find out how they are really living.

Jesus knew that this was what the Pharisees and scribes were doing. He confronted them with their deception by saying, "Woe unto you, scribes and Pharisees, hypocrites! for ye are like unto whited sepulchres, which indeed appear beautiful outward, but are within full of dead men's bones, and of all uncleanness" (Matt. 23:27).

Don't be a hypocrite! When you use God's name, let it be because you want to honor the God who has changed your life. Use His name purposefully, and live the Christian life vitally, praying that others will to want to serve Him as you do.

DISCUSSION QUESTIONS

What are some of the dishonoring things a young person may hide from his or her parents?

Can you think of a time when it was difficult for you to resist a temptation from your friends to do wrong?

Is it possible to be "less" than you should be and still think you are all right?

(▶ Parents, you know it is — don't let this slip by.)

Unit 3

How to Respond When Someone Dishonors God

Think about your name. It is used every time someone wants to speak about you to another person.

We use another person's name in three ways:

1. to identify
2. to honor
3. to dishonor that person

For example, maybe someone finds a book with your name in it. A friend of yours may tell that person, "Aaron is the boy who lives in the third house from the corner."

Another person may reply, "Aaron is a coward! He was probably running from someone when he dropped that book."

Yet a third person could respond: "I don't know

why you would say that! I've known Aaron since first grade, and he always stands up for what is fair or right!"

Which of these three people honored your name?

To honor someone's name we must know something about that person's character — we must know him or her personally. If we are going to be successful at honoring God's name, we must also know Him personally.

When a neighborhood playmate upsets you with his habit of saying, Oh, God! when something goes wrong, it will only embarrass him and make him angry if you say something about it in front of the other kids. But the next time you are alone with that playmate, ask him pleasantly, "Do you believe in God?"

He will probably look puzzled and reply, "I guess I do."

You might say: "I believe in Him because of the way He always helps our family. I ask Him to help me with school stuff, and I understand easier than I used to."

Then you can say: "The reason I wondered if you believed in Him is because sometimes you say Oh, God! I know you don't mean anything wrong, but my parents showed us where it says in the Bible not to use God's name in wrong ways. He wants us to use it for special things, like if we are in trouble. That's when we can call on His name, and ask Him to help us. If you will honor His name, He will help you too!"

How pleased God will be with you for speaking to your friend about His name.

Don't be discouraged if your friend doesn't listen to what you say. You will have planted a seed for God within that playmate's spirit. He may even make fun of you for telling him not to dishonor God, but the Holy Spirit will be able to deal with him within his heart because of the seed you planted.

DISCUSSION QUESTIONS

What are some of the things you know about God's character that can help you honor His name?

Can you illustrate a time when you pointed out to someone that he or she dishonored God's name? What did you say? How did he or she respond?

What are some of the ways to use God's name correctly?

Unit 4

Why God
Made the Sabbath

God made the Sabbath so that His people would have a day to rest from their labors (Ex. 20:10). It was a day to review all God had spoken to them, a time to meditate on His goodness.

In Jesus' day the Pharisees observed legalistic traditions regarding the Sabbath day, yet they failed to honor God in their hearts. Jesus knew their heart attitudes were wrong and that no matter how many legalistic traditions they observed with their actions, they were still dishonoring God — not just on the Sabbath but every day.

By pointing out their error, Jesus taught them, and us, that obeying God's rules with a pure heart is more important than going through the motions. When the Pharisees tried to entrap Jesus in their rules by condemning Him for healing a man on the Sabbath, Jesus replied:

What man is there among you who has one sheep, and if it falls into a pit on the Sabbath, will not lay hold of it, and lift it out? Of how much more value then is a man than a sheep? Therefore it is lawful to do good on the Sabbath (Matt. 12:11-12).

Jesus was telling us to keep our values straight. Right attitudes in our hearts will guide us into right actions.

Our memory verse tells us to *keep* God's day holy. Each one of us has a few things that we have tucked away in a safe place because they are precious to us. We may even call them *keepsakes*.

God says we are to *keep* the Sabbath rules. We are to appreciate His plan for a day of refreshing and worship. It doesn't need to be a "no fun" day. It can be a day when we do family things together such as playing games or going on a picnic. As a spiritual keepsake, it should be enjoyable for us — and pleasing to God. Let's try to be sure we keep the Lord's day as the best day in the week, one that shows others, and the Lord, how much we want to keep His day. It is a keepsake — a precious thing to us.

▓ The Hayford Heritage ▓

When my son Jim was the pastor of a local church, he planned the entire Sunday school program to coordinate with his sermon theme. This made it possible for the parents to discuss at home what they learned in church each Sunday. In this way each family was able to share God's Word together.

Unit 5

How Can We Keep His Day?

There are many ways that we can "remember the Sabbath day to keep it holy." We keep His day by faithfully attending church to learn from people who have been chosen to train us in God's ways and to teach us His Word.

We work or go to school Monday through Friday. For most people, Saturday is filled with other kinds of activities, thus making it a busy day or either work or fun. It is not "rest."

Besides the important time we take to enjoy corporate worship, let's try to make Sunday the day we set aside to enjoy rewarding activities. What are some things you can think of? Restful activities can restore our spirits and draw our attention to all that God has created for our enjoyment.

If at all possible, it should not be filled with working and shopping. How can we rearrange our schedule to make this a day of refreshing? (▶ Get serious about this and discuss fully.)

There is no law that says we cannot do anything on this day, but do you not think He would be pleased with us if we keep it a very special day?

It is also a good time to build relationships with other members of His body. (▶ Invite other families to spend the day with you.)

▶ Spend some time as a family planning creative ways to enjoy Sunday, while honoring God. Let each person plan a Sunday. Work out the details, and go for it!

DISCUSSION QUESTIONS

Can you name some of the traditional ways believers observe the Lord's day?

How can a teacher tell if a child attends Sunday school because he has to or because he wants to?

Can believers love God and still have a good time on Sunday?

▩ The Hayford Heritage ▩

It takes ingenuity and determination to keep learning competitive, fresh and *fun!*

We drew our children into each Bible story with questions and discussions. "I'm thinking of a lady in a story we have talked about before," my husband would begin. "Who do you think she might be?"

As our children responded, they would narrow the field: "Is it in the Old Testament? Was it in the history books? The first five books of the Bible? Was she in the book of Genesis?"

Finally one child would come up with the right answer. That child then continued by asking another question in greater detail about that particular Bible woman.

As we developed our style of teaching, our children began looking forward to the dinner hour when we would again play the game. Because we were continually reviewing all that they had learned, where their favorite stories were found in the Bible became as familiar as the stories themselves.

And with each story we taught, we answered to the question, "What does this story mean to the Hayford family?"

Because we were consistent in having these daily discussions, God became a normal part of our day and our lives.

Week 9

Respect Your Parents

Memory Verse

He who mistreats his father and chases away his mother is a son who causes shame and brings reproach.

Proverbs 19:26

Goal

To establish a pattern of respect within the family.

▦ The Hayford Heritage ▦

My husband and I often had foster children living in our home. When we had five or six children in our home at one time, it was the responsibility of an older child to teach or help a younger child. I would encourage this sense of responsibility by saying, "Tennie Jo always makes her bed so well, Karen. I am going to have her show you just how to do your bed. Then you can help her fold clothes as a thank-you."

Unit 1

The Meaning
Of Respect

Children's Prayer Focus

*Thank Jesus for the wonderful
parents He gave to you.*

Respect has many meanings. It can mean any of
the following: admiration, consideration, esteem,
regard, honor, appreciation, value or veneration.

Respect is something that parents earn by the
way they live their lives in front of their children.
It is something that should be part of every family's life together.

Many little boys can't wait to grow up to be just
like Daddy. How wonderful it is when this characteristic follows that little boy as he grows and
matures into a man. God smiles each time a
Christian daughter tells her friends, "I want to be
the kind of mother to my children that my mother
is to me."

Respect is admiration for the way your parents
handle the affairs of your home, as well as trust
and appreciation for the decisions your parents

make that affect your life.

Respect also means courtesy. It means happy and willing obedience to the things that are required of you as our children. It means a pleasant tone of voice and an agreeable countenance on both children and parents.

Disrespect should never be tolerated in a Christian family. Proverbs tells us, "A foolish [disrespectful] son is a grief to his father, and bitterness to her that bare him" (17:25).

God will not bless a disrespectful child. That person removes himself from the place of God's blessing.

God warned us about the end result of disrespect. There is no source of unhappiness within a family that is greater than the discord between parents and children. Whether we are obedient or disobedient will be very evident in the quality of life we enjoy together in our home.

If you understand why we have certain rules and practices, there should be no problem in accepting these things pleasantly.

God delights in a happily obedient heart.

DISCUSSION QUESTIONS

How can you show respect for your parents in each of the following ways?

1. Through admiration.

2. By being considerate.

3. By showing them esteem.

4. By regarding their words to you.

5. By giving them honor.

6. By appreciating something they do for you.

7. By letting them know you value their opinion.

8. By standing in awe of something they do or say (veneration).

Unit 2

God's Promises to Those Who Respect

God wants His children to be respectful. He wants us to respect and honor Him. But He also wants us to respect and honor each other — especially those who are in authority over us.

God has given some promises to those who show respect. Let's examine these promises.

1. A happy home and long life

> Solomon learned that his respect for his parents would be the key to a long life. He said, "For I was my father's son, tender and only beloved in the sight of my mother. He taught me also, and said unto me, Let thine heart retain my words: keep my commandments, and live" (Prov. 4:3-4, KJV).

2. A good relationship with your parents

Solomon also realized the importance of a good relationship with his parents. He tells us: "A wise son maketh a glad father" (Prov. 10:1, KJV).

3. Spiritual understanding

Spiritual discernment is vital for being successful in our spiritual walk. If we allow our parents and spiritual leaders to teach us about God, respecting their counsel and guidance, we will know what it takes to live for God. Proverbs tells us: "If thou wilt receive my words, and hide my commands within thee...then shalt thou understand the fear of the Lord, and find the knowledge of God" (Prov. 2:1,5, KJV).

4. Direction for life

As we respect God and allow His words to correct and reprove our errors, we will find clear direction for our lives. Proverbs 6 tells us, "When thou goest, it shall lead thee; when thou sleepest, it shall keep thee; and when thou awakest, it shall talk with thee. For the commandment is a lamp; and the law is light; and reproofs of instruction are the way of life" (6:22-23, KJV).

Respect brings rewards! Choose to be respectful.

DISCUSSION QUESTIONS

How can showing respect for your parents bring you a happy home and a long life?

Can you give a specific illustration of a time when being respectful helped you have a better relationship with your parents?

Why is it so important to be able to understand what the Bible says about living for God?

Has there been a time when one of God's rules helped you to correct an action or habit that you now know was wrong?

Unit 3

Learning Respect In the Home

Children's Prayer Focus

Thank God for the opportunity to learn to be respectful.

It is the responsibility of parents to train their children to live godly and righteous lives. When parents fulfill this responsibility in a loving and nurturing manner, children willingly submit to their parents' leadership and want to please them.

Every family, however, faces unique situations that must be worked out. That's why you must be taught to express your feelings in a courteous and respectful manner. Parents want only what is best for their children. Even though they must make decisions that are sometimes contrary to their children's desires, you can have confidence in the fact that God helps parents make wise decisions.

The Bible gives us the example of Moses, who had respect for God and therefore turned away from anything that kept him from obeying God. His life shows us the importance of learning to respect our parents' instructions.

> *By faith Moses, when he was come to years, refused to be called the son of Pharaoh's daughter; choosing rather to suffer affliction with the people of God, than to enjoy the pleasures of sin for a season; esteeming the reproach of Christ greater riches than the treasures in Egypt: for he had respect unto the recompense of the reward (Heb. 11:24-26).*

It's evident that Moses had been taught the difference between good and bad by his parents. When he no longer lived at home but had all the riches and pleasures of the palace of Egypt at his fingertips, he chose to do right. He respected the heritage of his parents.

Every day you will have to make choices like the one Moses had to make. There will be times when no one but you will know if you are being disrespectful to your parents' instructions. You may even have to "suffer affliction" by being respectful. Your peers may pressure you to "enjoy the pleasures of sin for a season."

It will be important for you to choose respect. God will reward the respect you show at home (and away from home) with joy and success and long life.

DISCUSSION QUESTIONS

What are some other ways that you believe our family can show respect and honor for one another?

Can you think of a decision that I made which you did not agree with but which you believed I had considered carefully?

What are some courteous and respectful ways for you to disagree with my decisions?

Unit 4

An Attitude Of Respect

Children's Prayer Focus

Pray for opportunities to show respect and kindness to each other.

Psychologists tell us that the root of much of the rebellion that is expressed by today's teenagers is the pain and disappointment of feeling unloved by their parents. These kids may *be* loved, but they *feel* unloved!

More than electronic toys, designer clothes and a big house with a swimming pool, children need — and want — the security of a home where love is genuinely and freely expressed. Here in our home, we are doing our best to nurture one another. We are forming a family bond that will be our support system for a lifetime.

One way to build this support system is for each one to do the tasks assigned him, knowing that they are deeply appreciated not only for the job done but also for the pleasant atmosphere that is maintained as we gladly do our share.

Because our life is very busy, we must plan ways to keep a right atmosphere in our home. Today we are going to talk about the things we do daily and find ways to help one another with our needs.

▶ Children who are raised from birth to show appreciation for each kindness shown to them, and to demonstrate kindness to their family members, will rarely become rebellious teenagers.

▶ *Parent Tip*

In advance of this unit of study, prepare a printed schedule for each family member. Include the tasks each must do daily (such as meal preparation, homework, laundry, housecleaning and so on). Pass these out to each family member.

Make sure everyone keeps discussion time in their schedule. I strongly suggest evening meal time. It is by far the least intrusive time.

Today, as you gather for this discussion time, begin by saying, "My busy-ness and stress is no excuse for being angry or short-tempered with you. I need your forgiveness if I have been at fault. And your busy life is no reason to be sassy, grumpy or disrespectful."

Do we need to change anything in our various schedules to make sure we can go on sharing God's Word each day? (Talk about it.)

Tip to parents — especially single parents.

Although you have read about the number of people in my family, and probably figured out that I've been around for "countless ages," do not assume that giving faithful attention to spiritual training is impossible today. When it comes to being God's kind of parent, raising God's kind of children, you can expect it to be a time-consuming task.

Being a fairly creative thinker, I have always been able to take as many shortcuts as the law would allow. But the bad news is that the major "cuts" — what you have to give up to make time for your kids — will involve things you really enjoyed! Maybe you are gifted and even sought after, but right now (unless you are teaching your children to perfect these skills) these skills probably need to take a lower place on your priority list. (You'll stage a comeback.)

Your children will be gone before you know it, and you can't imagine how painful the results of a "half-way" job can be — after it is too late to fix it!

The lifetime relationship you are setting in place with them, however, is worth it all. Kids are open to anything you have to teach them if they are happy. Because at times you will have to use discipline to get your point across, learning to discipline using reason instead of anger is probably one of the most effective skills to perfect.

Deuteronomy 6:4-7 works — and is rewarding.

Unit 5

An Attitude
Of Gratitude

Children's Prayer Focus

*Thank God for the kind things other
people have done for you.*

Respect for parents must be very important since
God grants a special reward to the person who
complies.

Not all parents are easy to respect. That is defi-
nitely a result of disobedience on their part. If you
have a parent who does not serve God and is a
failure as a parent, God will highly honor you if
you show respect to this parent anyway.

Somewhere along the line, something happened
to the person who cannot be a good parent. Ask
Jesus to help you feel sorry for that parent because
he or she is so badly broken. Parents can change
as their children pray for them.

Think of anything you could thank that parent
for, no matter how small. Tell them you remember
that good thing they did.

As we conclude our week's study on respect, we are going to make and exchange gratitude cards. Each of us will draw the name of a family member and make a card. (▶ Put each person's name in a bowl and allow each person to draw one name. Provide paper, markers, scissors and other craft supplies appropriate for making cards.)

On the front of your card, create a picture or saying that expresses your thankfulness for the person for whom you are making your card.

On the inside of our cards we are going to make an acrostic using the word *gratitude*. For each letter of the word, write something about that person for which you are thankful.

The following example will help you to think of your own acrostic:

G good times together
R running to the store when I needed paper
A apples in my lunch every day
T taking time to take me to McDonald's
I increasing my weekly allowance
T tacos, turkey, tortellini and trays of cookies
U understanding my moods
D dusting my room when I was too busy
E every day, because she loves me

It is important to train your children from birth to show appreciation for each kindness shown them. They should not be allowed to ignore another's kind act toward them or to fall into the routine of sibling bickering and arguing.

You should also lead them to a genuine understanding of your commitment to help each child become the best person possible. Help them to understand the unique contribution each family member makes to the family relationship.

When friction or disrespect arises, sit down and determine the cause and deal with it. By your consistent, close adherence to making your children know you will not permit discord, your children will learn to work out their differences peaceably.

Teach your children to respect the family rules. Be consistent in requiring obedience. When discipline is required, discipline in love.

Take time with each child each evening to discuss his or her individual needs. Pray together, asking God to forgive your failures and to guide you into His perfect plan for each member of the family.

Pray a lot! Even a rebellious heart can be recaptured for God through repentance and love.

Week 10

Do Not Harbor Anger

Memory Verse

But I say to you, love your enemies, bless those who curse you, do good to those who hate you, and pray for those who spitefully use you and persecute you.

Matthew 5:44

Goal
To understand the different methods and attitudes that can be defined as "murder" within the heart.

Prayer Focus
Pray pointedly for each of your children to be willing to examine his or her feelings about others. Pray with your children daily for a heart attitude of love and sympathetic understanding of those who are hard to enjoy.

▶ Be sure your children understand fully how it is possible to "kill" a person's opportunities, and thus spoil their lives — even though they are still living. This is done by character assassination.

Unit 1

A World Without Rules

Children's Prayer Focus

Ask God to reveal any heart attitudes that are wrong.

The world is not living by God's rules. And worse yet, not much is being done about it! There was a time when the laws of our nation were based upon the laws of the Bible. That is not so anymore. Can you name some evidences that we are living in a world without rules?

Acts of hatred, violence and murder are committed continually throughout our world. Many lives are lost every day because of outright acts of murder. But other deaths occur because of acts of violence that society fails to label as murder, such as abortion, euthanasia and "justifiable homicide" in spouse abuse cases. (▶ Be prepared to explain these terms if your children do not understand them.) In still other cases, death does not actually occur but is contemplated and desired because of anger and hatred within the heart.

God places a priceless value on every person's life. No one has the right to take the life of another. Jesus expanded our understanding of murder by saying, "You have heard that it was said to those of old, 'You shall not murder, and whoever murders will be in danger of the judgment.' But I say to you that whoever is angry with his brother without a cause shall be in danger of the judgment" (Matt. 5:21-22).

Most of us cannot even imagine being tempted to murder another person. But we may have been guilty of harboring grudges against our friends or family members many times. It is important that we learn to see the best in another person instead of looking at the things about that person that upset us or cause us to be angry inside our hearts.

Murder begins within the heart: "For out of the heart proceed...murders" (Matt. 15:19). Murder is as much an attitude of the heart as it is an action of the will. It is the work of Satan. We must recognize his power at work in a world that has chosen to be disobedient to God's rules.

Remember that God always deals with our heart. This scripture illustrates God's working in our heart: "Search me, O God, and know my heart...and see if there is any wicked way in me" (Ps. 139:23-24).

DISCUSSION QUESTIONS

How can a continuing feud lead to murderous thoughts within the heart?

What should I do if I hold great anger in my heart?

What are some ways people lose their lives — ways the law allows?

Unit 2

God's
"Do Nots"

Children's Prayer Focus

Pray for the courage to obey God's "do-nots" in every situation.

The only commandments that tell us *not* to do something deal with three things we have known not to do since we were very young: murder, steal and lie. We will take a look at stealing and lying later. This week we are dealing with murder — an act which, if committed, will change the entire course of our life.

Taking another life, or counting another's life as less important than our own, takes a toll that cannot be erased during the perpetrator's lifetime. Even if the courts grant freedom and God grants forgiveness, murder can never be erased from the memory. It is terrible to realize the sin of which the human heart is capable if we do not guard the heart diligently.

David carried remorse for his sinful act of murder against the husband of Bathsheba for the rest of his days.

Unpremeditated murder is often the result of hidden anger. Jesus dealt with the dangers of anger in His Sermon on the Mount (see Matt. 5:21-22). Undealt with, it can lead us straight to hell!

Putting God's Word in our hearts and spirits can help us deal with anger. His Word is intended to be a fortress of life-saving truth about God's plan to save our souls. All His admonitions should be grasped as surely as we would grasp a rope thrown to us if we fell overboard on an ocean trip. He helps us deal with our angry thoughts so they cannot become a tool for Satan to use against us.

Let's look at some of His admonitions about anger. How do these verses apply to your life?

> *Make no friendship with an angry man, and with a furious man do not go (Prov. 22:24).*

> *An angry man stirs up strife, and a furious man abounds in transgressions (Prov. 29:22).*

> *Do not hasten in your spirit to be angry, for anger rests in the bosom of fools (Eccl. 7:9).*

> *Whoever is angry with his brother without a cause shall be in danger of the judgment (Matt. 5:22).*

DISCUSSION QUESTIONS

What emotion is beneath most unpremeditated acts of murder?

Why do you think God's Word advises us to avoid friendships with angry people?

What tool is available to us to keep Satan from trapping us with our anger?

Can you give an example of a time when something you knew about God helped you to overcome the anger you were feeling toward another person?

Murderous Thoughts Are a Concern to God

Children's Prayer Focus

Ask Jesus to reveal any hidden anger in your heart.

We have already mentioned this week that murder begins within the heart. Today we want to see that although hatred may never become an act of murder, it will certainly rob you of a happy heart and create moodiness.

In the book of Galatians, the apostle Paul lists the works of the flesh. Many of these sinful actions and emotions eventually lead to murder in an effort to cover up some wickedness that was allowed to become a part of one's life.

Lists in the Bible usually have significance in they way they "pile up," one thing leading to another. Satan is a hard taskmaster and will try to ensnare you whenever he can. So for your own peace of mind, keep your heart clean.

In the fifth chapter of Galatians, the Bible talks about the "words of the flesh." In order to help you understand it better, let me put it in my own words.

Thoughts and actions that are unclean or wicked, having to do with sexual behavior both inside and outside of marriage, are completely forbidden by God. Such things are an abomination to Him.

But look at the other things He puts in the same group. These are things He wants nothing to do with:

(▶ Explain where necessary.)

1. Outbursts of anger
2. Pursuing false doctrines
3. Selfish ambition
4. Witchcraft and fortune-telling
5. Arguing with established authority
6. Drunkenness (or drug use)
7. Hatred
8. Envy and jealousy

Sometimes we think certain sins are not as bad as others. We often say things such as: "Well, that is really awful, but at least it is not like — ."

The truth is, sin is sin. It is choosing to go Satan's way. But Jesus prompts us to choose His way. Are you listening to Him?

DISCUSSION QUESTIONS

How can you "kill" your own conscience?
(▶ Think of the effects of what you watch
or listen to.) What would happen if:

1. Adultery and fornication appeared
   in a movie you were watching?

2. Obscene or vulgar behavior (uncleanness and lewdness) became common on
   the school grounds?

3. A friend became involved in the occult?

4. You express hatred and argue with your
   brother?

5. Jealousy and anger overwhelmed you?

6. Selfish ambition and envy tempted you
   to commit wrong actions?

7. Some acquaintances at school invited
   you to their drunken, wild parties?

Unit 4

Antidote for Hateful Attitudes: Love

Children's Prayer Focus

Thank Jesus for your friends and family — by name.

To get rid of bad heart attitudes, we need God to reveal His antidote. It is love.

> *You have heard that it was said, "You shall love your neighbor and hate your enemy." But I say to you, love your enemies, bless those who curse you, do good to those who hate you, and pray for those who spitefully use you and persecute you (Matt. 5:43-44).*

Our memory verse is clear about the attitude of Jesus concerning love. He commanded us to love others — even our enemies.

Loving your enemies is not an easy thing to do. There are oceans of emotions between the words "hate your enemy" and "love your enemies" in that verse. Yet we know God never asks us to do something that is impossible. When someone at school curses you because you won't give him the answers to the exam, bless him. Say, "I can't cheat and give you the answers, but I'd be happy to study with you during study hall today."

When another girl on your basketball team says she hates you because you were chosen co-captain instead of her, do good to her by passing the ball to her for the winning lay-up instead of making the basket yourself.

God shares with us a secret for success in our memory verse. He says to pray for these kinds of people. Prayer is a powerful thing! It can cause that girl to reconsider how she feels about you. You may discover you have a new friend. I have seen that happen! (▶ Be prepared to share such an experience from your own life.)

It concerns me to deal with a truth like thi, and to realize how seldom we even try to do it. Let's look for something really good in a person we don't like very much, and share it with each other. (▶ Let each person name the one they are going to be praying for.)

DISCUSSION QUESTIONS

Can you give an example of a time when you used the antidote of love on someone who disliked you?

What situations are you facing now in which love is needed?

Discuss how the following situations could be used as opportunities to show love to another person:

- mowing your unpleasant neighbor's lawn for free

- leaving playtime to cheerfully run an errand for your mother

- offering to stay after school to help your crabby teacher

- being willing to be the water boy on the team even though you missed the cut unfairly

Can you name some other times when you were able to show love to someone unlovable?

Unit 5

What Love Is

The Bible says, "God is love" (1 John 4:8).
Our author illustrates how she learned to understand God's perspective on love.

▦ The Hayford Heritage ▦

As a young Christian, I believed the Bible simply because God said it was true. It wasn't until I became a parent that I got a better perspective on the love of God that the Bible described.

I was perplexed as I read some of God's drastic judgments on wicked nations. I knew His patience extended far longer than we can imagine, yet it was obvious there were times when He responded to the sins of people with, "You've gone far enough!"

Then one day my two-year-old son stamped

his foot and screamed emphatically, "No!"

It was as if God whispered in my ear, "The Philistines are coming!" I was galvanized into action. My dearly loved boy came at me with sword and shield, and God told me, "This has to be done away with completely."

My son had been playing with my neighbor's son — a little boy who practically ruled the household. "No" was a primary part of his vocabulary. When I arrived in her yard to bring my son home for his nap, my neighbor called to her son, "You better have your nap now, too. When you wake up — "

That was as far as she got. Her son began running from her, screaming "No! No! *No!*" at the top of his lungs. "I'm not going to take a nap! I don't like to take a nap! I am going to stay here and play with my cars!"

As I piloted my own son across the lawn, he looked over his shoulder with great interest. This was not the first time he had seen such a performance. But I had not realized the influence it was having. As we neared our porch, I heard my neighbor say, "Doesn't Tommy love Mommy anymore?"

"No! I hate you! You are a *bad* Mommy!" her young son responded with great emotion.

She opened her arms wide and lovingly cooed: "All right, then. If Mommy promises to be good, will you just come in the house and lay down on the couch while I play your favorite record for you? Mommy will sit right there with you — you don't have to take an old nap!"

Not wanting him to hear all this, I said, "Let's go on in the house."

My own son stood glaring at me. A disobedient *"No!"* rang across the yard. I picked him up and took him into the house. Standing him on the kitchen table, eye-to-eye, I said, "What did you say?"

The shield and sword flew off into space. A very insecure little boy now stood before me. "Did I say...*no?*"

With the Lord prompting, I continued, "You tell *me* what you said."

"I think I said no," he whispered, tears welling up in both eyes.

(Another whisper reached me from heaven.) "Tell me how you said it, son," I responded.

His tears flowed freely. "I can't say it that big, Mamma, it will hurt my mouth!"

By now I was turning to jelly. I held him in my arms. Even though I could see he was repentant, God prodded me one more time. "Whom the Lord loves, He chastens" (Heb. 12:6).

Then, in mercy to me, He spoke to me as my child said, "I think I need some spanks!"

Love not only blesses; it requires of itself a willingness to pay the cost of doing right — whatever that cost may be.

Week 11

Keep Your Love For One Partner

Memory Verse

Now Jacob loved Rachel...So Jacob served seven years for Rachel, and they seemed only a few days to him because of the love he had for her.

Genesis 29:18,20

Goal

To establish the importance of the bonds of love within marriage and family.

▶ This lesson presents God's ideal for marriage — two people who love each other and remain married for life. It needs to be the goal set for your children and the pattern of training for their future. If your home has been broken by divorce, your children understand your pain more than you know. Talk with them about your misunderstanding of God's Word before you married, if that was the case. Emphasize God's willingness to help your family now — whatever the situation may be. Ask what is most difficult for *them*, and how you might help.

Unit 1

Love Makes the World Go Round

Today, our author shares her own experience in learning to build a marriage that is pleasing to God.

▦ The Hayford Heritage ▦

I had gathered my children, packed their clothing and toys, packed my clothing and a few treasured belongings, and left our home. I left a note saying why I had gone. Within a week an attorney had mailed the notification of my application for divorce. Six weeks later I returned to that city for the court hearing.

As I started up the steps to the courtroom, my husband met me. I could scarcely believe my eyes — he looked absolutely desolate. He had lost a great deal of weight. He had quit his job and returned to drinking.

My father, who had never approved of our

marriage, was with me on those steps and attempted to hurry me into the courtroom. But I heard another voice, God clearly spoke to my heart with these words: "If you do this, your husband will never make it."

I had never seen my husband weep before. He begged me to forgive his infidelity and give him another chance. He had lined up another job in his home state and promised to get himself together if I would just return to him.

To my father's disgust, I said, "All right. You get settled and get a place for us. When you have done that, send for us and we will come."

I didn't want to return to him. I was wounded to the core of my being. I knew my family would oppose our reconciliation, but I was afraid *not* to do what God was asking me to do. Even then, it was years before I was able to understand that it was not lack of love for me, but much deeper insecurities that had tricked him.

But with those years, spiritual maturity brought healing — healing for my husband, who had no self-esteem as a result of a terribly destructive childhood. Though only a very young believer, my husband had a genuine passion for the Word of God. The devil feared that passion and tried to kill it by destroying our marriage.

And those years brought healing for my stinging pride and deep hurt. I too had been too young in the Lord to see things clearly. Had I followed my own destructive path toward divorce, my children would never have ended up as they did. No doubt they would have been good citizens, but they have become much more than that. Each one has had great spiritual impact in God's kingdom.

My husband and I determined to find a way to share my husband's love for God's Word with our children. He was a devoted father, wanting his children to experience the stability and emotional security he never had in his own childhood. He was demanding, but giving.

We shared forty-eight years of growing together, with our marriage in a constant state of *becoming*. If I had to experience the difficulties again to see the harvest that has been gleaned, I would do so without a moment's hesitation.

The spiritual impact my husband had on our children was the major ingredient of the mix. My major contribution was listening to God when I really wanted to punish my husband.

There is no perfect marriage. But God's perfect plan is the solution to life's painful problems.

Unit 2

What if Love Is Broken?

Children's Prayer Focus

Thank God for loving and comforting you as your heavenly Father.

God's Word tells us that God hates divorce because it hurts people, and He *loves* people! "For the Lord God of Israel says that He hates divorce, for it covers one's garment with violence" (Mal. 2:16).

God loves men and women who have divorced! And he loves children who have had to face their parents' divorce.

God is love. He feels our human pain. He has a strong desire to see families trouble-free and content. This is the nature and disposition of our Creator. He knows that in today's world divorce is growing like a weed. It chokes out the beauty of a godly family just as a weed snuffs out the life of a delicate rose.

The book of Hebrews gives us an illustration of the effect of divorce on a family:

See to it that no one misses the grace of God and that no bitter root grows up to cause trouble and defile many (12:15, NIV).

Divorce is a bitter root growing up and defiling many in our world today. It reaches into future generations, and the chain of its curse must be broken — and can be through the grace and forgiveness of God.

The New Testament records only two times when Jesus mentioned divorce (see Matthew 19 and Mark 10). But something interesting happens each time. Jesus first speaks to the adults — probably many of whom were parents — about the destructiveness of divorce. Immediately after He finishes, He calls the little children to come to Him. He takes them upon His lap and shows them how much He loves them. They had heard His words of admonition to their parents. Perhaps some of them knew from experience how painful it was to go through a divorce. Now — more importantly — they were experiencing the healing love of Jesus.

As a Christian family we must take care to protect ourselves against the enemy's attempt to destroy our family, and allow ourselves to be to those around us a pattern of a family healed by the beauty of God's love.

DISCUSSION QUESTIONS

(▶ Be sure the questions you ask today fit the situation in your family.)

Has the thought of divorce ever frightened you? Why?

Can you describe the way a divorce must feel to someone who experiences it?

How do you think God's love and grace can wipe out the effects of divorce in someone's life?
(▶ see 2 Cor. 5:17 and 1 John 1:9)

Unit 3

Be
Equally Yoked

There are two interesting biblical references to a yoke. One is:

> *Do not be unequally yoked together with unbelievers. For what fellowship has right-eousness with lawlessness? (2 Cor. 6:14).*

A yoke is a wooden beam that binds two oxen together so they work together more efficiently. Two mismatched oxen, perhaps one young and strong and the other old and weak, would not be an efficient team. Nor would one high-spirited, temperamental ox enjoy spending the day with a slow, methodical, placid ox. God warns us to be careful to choose a like-minded mate. We should consider that warning carefully in order to avoid becoming "unequally yoked" *before* we agree to marry another person. There will be enough little differences to iron out, such as which way the toilet paper goes on the roller or who gets which side of the bed.

Spiritual differences are far different. For example, if my mate is comfortable with "church attendance if it is convenient" before we marry, that attitude is not likely to change after marriage.

Remember too, it is just as easy to be unequally yoked to another believer as it is if you marry a non-believer. A good marriage is built on a sound friendship in which we have explored each other's goals and dreams for the future.

Let Jesus be the yoke gladly borne by each of you as you enter into the relationship of marriage.

That's where a second verse about a yoke comes in:

> *Take My yoke upon you and learn from Me, for I am gentle and lowly in heart, and you will find rest for your souls. For My yoke is easy and My burden is light (Matt. 11:29-30).*

We must yoke ourselves together for marriage with God's yoke! He will gently lead us to build a godly marriage. Our home will be a haven of rest with His help.

A healthy love relationship between parents strongly affects the lives of our children. Kids gain great security from such a home.

The marriage relationship involves a complete giving of one's very self and the receiving of the "self" of another. When God said, "It is not good that man should be alone" (Gen. 2:18), in essence He was saying, "It is wonderful for man to have someone with whom he is 'at one.'"

Familial love and acceptance is the very stuff of which character and self-confidence are made. Children born into homes where the parents are not happy with one another are affected deeply. It is impossible for couples who are in conflict to create the atmosphere God wants to permeate a home.

Parental rifts devastate children. Childhood loyalties are taxed beyond their limits. Such stress produces ambivalent feelings about marriage when these children become adults. They lack confidence that their own marriages will be better. They are very fearful of making the commitment to marry.

God said to choose one partner for an entire lifetime. This choice begins with dating. If you have established a good relationship with your children, they will choose carefully and will care about your input. Be prayerful to be sure you are gracious and fair. Train them to be prepared for marriage — spiritually, emotionally, physically and permanently!

Unit 4

God
Created Families

"Family" is God's idea. It has always been His desire to be a part of each family's life. Our children are the next generation of hope for a hopeless and dying world. Their basic training is to be given at home — by their parents.

A godly home is not a pious, overly-religious place. Religion stifles. Jesus brings life. Jesus also brings nurturing and warmth, morality and contentment.

All living creatures learn by modeling. Imprinting begins to take place from birth, and the child who is welcomed and loved wants to emulate the ones who gave him life.

Parents in a truly godly home live by God's rules and enjoy Him as a loving Father. Children in such a home are a gift from, and to, God (Ps. 127:3).

Whatever your situation may be (one parent in

the home, one parent with grandparents or, perhaps, two working parents who use day care), any of these more difficult arrangements are cases where the need is greater than ever for you to have this regular spiritual input with your kids. There is no situation that sets God's mandate aside.

Hopefully, there is at least agreement among the adults involved regarding the children's spiritual needs and a feeling of family when everyone is at home.

How does our family fulfill God's plan for a Christian family? How can we arrange things so we have this special time together without stress? What are some creative ways for our family to spend more time together?

FAMILY ACTIVITY

Have a memory verse review and allow each family member to tell which verse he or she understands best.

Satan begins to make his bid for your children when they're in the cradle. Tantrums, pity parties, whining and excuses are indications that you are failing as a parent. It is never too late to change. When *you* know it is not appropriate for your child to do something, it does not matter how many others are doing it.

Give your children choices within a range of acceptable responses. From their earliest years, explain why you do not allow certain music in the home, why you carefully screen the places you allow them to go and why you require them to get your approval regarding friendships. Establish boundaries for your children's activities.

Make sure you provide them with many opportunities to attend good concerts, plays or movies; to make their friends feel welcome in your home; and to experience fun, happy family times together.

Help your kids to get *hooked* on God and His will for their lives. No one discards easily something that is enjoyable and profitable. Their relationship with God should be like that.

Admit your failures to your children. Model a life that is constantly being "conformed to the image of Christ."

Unit 5

The Family
That Plays Together

▶ Parent Tip

In sharing God's Word with your children, constant review is the secret of success. I have suggested that you set aside monthly sessions for this purpose. We have called it "Game Night." A sure way to prevent this activity from becoming boring for the kids is to have them ask the questions. As you begin doing this, listen for really pertinent questions. Make a note of the question and who asked it. This will be the basis for a second game, which you will use in the future.

Whenever a correct answer is given, the person who answered becomes "it." If you have very small children, let them answer, but they should not be "it" for a while. They do learn quickly and will soon come up with questions of their own.

As you begin Game Night, keep things moving by deciding whether the next question should be on the same subject, or if it is time to think about another lesson.

From the beginning, insist that the answer include the Bible reference from which the question was taken.

A good beginning would be the memory verses. Say: "I'm thinking of a verse that tells us how God feels about our family. Where is it, and how does it say He feels?"

The first child to the left may respond: "I know how He feels, but I forgot where it is."

"Sorry, you have to tell that first," you answer.

The next person in the circle may ask, "Is it in Deuteronomy?"

To which you reply, "Yes, but where?"

Since that person received a yes, he continues: "It's in the fifth chapter, verse twenty-nine."

"Right," you answer, "what does it say?"

If the same person can recite the verse correctly, he now becomes "it" and may ask the next question.

When you have accumulated ten or twelve good questions (writing down who formed the questions), play the game "Remember when — ?" For this game the parent asks all the questions from their notes for this game.

"Remember when John asked us, 'What are the thirty-seven words that tell it all?' Well, John knows that answer, so he can't play this round. Mary was the one who gave the answer to John's question. She's out too! Who can tell me the right answer now?"

Another game is "It Has Been Said." Jesus used this phrase (Matt. 5:31; Luke 4:12). "It" thinks of the topic of his question and says, "It has been said that he had a leather belt."

The first responder may get a no. The person who is "it" then gives another clue: "It has been said that he lived alone, away from the city."

The next responders may ask: "Is he in the Old Testament?" "Did he know Jesus?" then "Is it John the Baptist?"

The person who guesses the answer correctly becomes "it."

It is a good idea to pursue a thorough review of each Bible character you choose. For example, when you review John the Baptist, you would want to include questions about his odd diet and the time he heard God's voice from out of the sky.

You can include questions from these lessons, and also study parts of the Bible that are being studied in your children's Sunday school lessons. Just be sure each issue dealt with is accurately remembered. Include what is actually being said and the exact location for the story in the Bible.

Week 12

Love Goes On

Memory Verse

Be kindly affectionate to one another with brotherly love, in honor giving preference to one another.

Romans 12:10

Goal
To develop creative methods for strengthening the family unit in a world that often threatens it.

Prayer Focus
During this week, focus on the individual and family needs of your unique family situation. Continue developing creative ways to spend more time together.

▶ Use the opportunity this week to strengthen the family bonds. Concentrate on the special contribution of each family member. Express appreciation for each person, guiding your children to build on the framework of love.

Unit 1

Love Is Commanded

In an earlier unit, we learned that Jesus is our commander, and our heart is His command post.

Our commander gave us a new commandment in John 13:35: "A new commandment I give to you, that you love one another." He spoke those words to His people three times — in the above verse adding the words, "as I have loved you."

His love for us is our "measuring cup" of how we are to love others. How much do you think He loves *our* family? How has He shown special love for you personally?

This commandment is hard to keep. Often we overlook our weakness in loving others because it is overshadowed by personal judgmentalism, jealousy or envy. Unless we are healed of our shortcomings in these areas, our ability to love others as Christ loves us is sorely limited.

The following story illustrates this point.

Several members of a Sunday school class complained to the teacher about one of the little boys who attended. "His clothes are always dirty," said one little girl. "He always spends the money he has on himself instead of putting it in the offering," another stated. Two other kids joined in with, "He cusses at the other kids" and "He takes more than his share when there are treats."

The teacher remembered the day when Timmy, the boy they were talking about, had knelt with her and received Jesus as his personal Savior. She recalled that he had seemed to fit in better while he was still in the primary department.

One Sunday the teacher and her husband offered to drive Timmy home. That day he had stated to her emphatically, "I'm never coming back to *this* place!"

"Can we call your house and see if it's OK for you to go to lunch with us first?" the teacher asked.

"It don't matter," Timmy responded immediately. "My mom is workin', and I ain't got no dad — well, I *do*, but we don't know where he is."

As they talked over hamburgers and french fries, the teacher's husband asked Timmy, "Are you friends with any of the kids in Sunday school?"

"I don't like any of them kids," Timmy blurted out angrily. "They think they're better than everybody else — all dressed up like it's Easter or something."

The teacher realized that none of the kids would respond favorably to Timmy even if he did try to be friends with them.

Timmy continued, "You know, when anybody hates your guts...." Then he laughed nervously and said, "Sometimes I just cuss at 'em when they whisper about me. I know that ain't right. My mom pops me one if I cuss at home. My mom wants me to be a Christian."

The boy ate ravenously. As they finished eating, he dug in his pockets and pulled out a dime. "I can pay part. My mom always gives me a dime for the offering, but the kids laugh because it ain't much. So I don't give it no more."

Unknowingly, Timmy had addressed most of the charges that had been brought against him!

Who would be to blame if this boy quit attending Sunday school? (▶ Spend some time discussing this story.) What can our church do about the "Timmys" we know? What can we do personally?

Timmy would act more lovable if he was loved more. We need to consider the circumstances of another person's life before we judge them as being unworthy of our love. Jesus loved unconditionally. He found ways to express His love to everyone — regardless of what they looked like or how they acted. We must do the same.

Unit 2

Love Is Demonstrated

Children's Prayer Focus

Tell God some ways you want to demonstrate love.

Today we are going to take a look at an example of love from the life of our author.

▣ The Hayford Heritage ▣

When I was about nine years old, my mother gave me the responsibility of ironing the pillow cases and handkerchiefs for our family. She showed me how to get all the threads in the material straight and how to make the folds just right. I liked to iron.

One summer day my friend called early in the morning to tell me she would pick me up at 10:00 a.m. to go swimming.

When I sat down at the table for breakfast, my mother said, "Dolores, be sure you get your part of the ironing done in plenty of time to go swimming today."

After breakfast I went down to the family room in the basement of our house. Summers were hot in Arizona, and we always ironed in the nice, cool basement early in the morning. While I waited for the iron to warm up, I started working on a jigsaw puzzle that was on the table. I became so engrossed in the puzzle that before I knew it, it was 9:15!

Because the steam iron had not yet been invented, my mother had already sprinkled the handkerchiefs with water and rolled each one up, ready to be ironed. Hurriedly, I grabbed the first handkerchief and began ironing. But instead of laying the pieces on the ironing board neatly as I had been taught, I folded each hanky first and ironed only the *outside* parts. Nervously, I watched the stairs, afraid my mother would come down and discover what I was doing.

Something began to churn inside as Satan launched his attack. (This usually happens when we purposely disobey God's rules.) I thought, Most of my friends don't have to iron! My mother should be doing this ironing herself. I had forgotten completely that it was I who had begged her to teach me to iron.

I was finishing my last bit of deceit at ten minutes to ten when Mom called, "Honey, you'd better stop and get ready to go swimming. You can finish this afternoon." I turned off the iron and put the pillow cases in the linen closet. Then I ran to my mother's bedroom and put the handkerchiefs in the drawer, grabbed my bathing suit and ran out the door.

Five days later, Mom called me to the linen closet. "Do you smell anything funny?"

I did, but I had never heard of mildew. I had forgotten all about my "speed ironing" which had left the handkerchiefs and pillow cases still damp when I put them away. My mother shook out first one pillow case and then another. Big, black smudges of mildew were all over each one. Even after bleaching, the pillow cases looked like they had the plague. I wept every time I ironed her handkerchiefs. My mom loved pretty handkerchiefs — but they were no longer pretty!

I apologized to her over and over. Each time she said, "Well, there are plenty of nice ones left for when I am with someone who sees them." (She knew it was good for me to live with my sin for a while!) She did not replace the eight mildew-stained pillow cases for several weeks, so I had to face the results of my disobedience all that time.

I loved her most of all the day we threw them away! Usually we put old things in a "rag bag" to use for cleaning chores. But Mamma said, "We've seen enough of these!" and threw them away.

Unit 3

Home Is
A Refuge

There are two portions of Scripture that allow us to take a close look at God's design for parenting.

Today we are going to look first at the role of the father as illustrated in the life of the deacon described in 1 Timothy 3:8-12. (▶ Ask one of your children to read this portion of Scripture.)

These are qualities of a Christian father:

- reverent
- honest
- not a drinker
- not greedy for money (or materialism)
- pure in action
- blameless
- a spiritual leader at home
- happily married
- successful in his discipline of his children
- rules well at home.

Then in Proverbs 31:10-31 we find the qualities of a Christian mother. (▶ Read this scripture.)

These are qualities of a Christian mother:

- trusted by her mate
- supports her husband emotionally
- works willingly
- is a good cook
- takes good care of her family's needs
- is able to handle money well
- is strong in character
- completes the work at home
- gives to the needy
- plans for emergencies
- can find a way to give financial support from home if necessary
- is a wise counsel
- treats her family with kindness
- is not idle
- is loved and appreciated by her husband and family.

Whether or not your home is headed up by two loving parents, I am sure you, as the parent, desire above all things that your children have such a home when they marry.

If this is the case with you, and your children are eight or older, talk with them about the condition of families in our nation. Discuss things that are acceptable in our society today but are not what

God intended them to be.

Explain your own situation as honestly as you can, and how — had you known how to choose a life partner who would also have valued the principles you now embrace — things might have been different.

Be frank. Biology is biology. We all reach an age where we want a special person to love us. If we do not know God's standards, we can be carried away by all sorts of wrong reasons to marry. You will be blessed to find how sympathetic and understanding kids can.

Tell them how much you want for them to have the benefits you have been reading about in the lesson today. Let them talk about it. Ask them how they think all of you could work together with God's help to create the atmosphere that should prevail in a godly home.

If there is anything of merit to be said about the missing parent, be sure to share this with the children. The other parent did not set out to be a failure, and as God's family, we need to be sensitive to their failure as well as to our own problems.

Unit 4

Creating a Home When Both Parents Work

Gene and Vicki Johnston are a unique couple. They have both chosen to continue working, but they have strong feelings about parental obligations. They created a way to have the "best of both worlds."

It has not been easy, but they spend themselves without regret to provide their children (they now have three) with everything they would normally receive if there were only one working parent. Vicki wanted very much to continue in her position as an inner-city elementary school teacher. Gene knew how much she had done for the children in the school and wanted to support her in her dream.

When their first child was born, Vicki took a year's leave of absence so she could nurse her child and be the primary caregiver for the baby in this very important period of life.

Gene is a research chemist. During the first pregnancy, and the first year of the child's life, he spent time looking into laboratories that operated around the clock. By the time baby Debra was a year old, he had located and transferred to such a job.

They had also worked with Debra's schedule, so that when she was one year old she awoke at 5 and ate breakfast with her mother at 7. By the time Daddy came home at 7:30, Mom was ready to leave for school.

Daddy and Debbie would play or go grocery shopping during the next couple of hours, and when it was time for her morning nap, Gene would go to bed. Around 11:30, his sister, who wanted a little part-time job, would let herself in and start the chores.

She prepared lunch for Debbie and took her out for fresh air and a stroll, bringing her home around 2:00. Gene woke up at about 4:00, just as Vicki was getting home. The next two hours were spent in the family room (a habit that continues even now with three children). Debbie uses this time to grade papers but is never too busy to stop and be involved with one of the kids.

Gene is a reader and spends a lot of time in these late afternoon hours either helping with homework or reading a book of his own.

Part of his sister's job is to have dinner ready to put in the oven, vegetables prepared and a salad made. At 5:30 Vicki sets the table with the children's help, and finalizes the dinner preparations. They eat at 6:00, and this family *does* have their time with the Lord at the dinner table. They love it, and all the kids are doing remarkably well.

Gene helps the children get into night clothes while Vicki clears up from the meal. Then they spend an hour watching a television show or a video, or playing games. At 8:00 P.M. the kids are put to bed, and Vicki and Gene have a couple of hours to themselves.

Yes, it is a full schedule. No, they do not do much of anything else. They are not stressed out, however. They know their limitations and their priorities. They have great weekends together.

At the present time they are teaching the kids to swim on Saturday afternoons. On Sunday they attend church both morning and evening.

If both adults have to work in your family, please consider the example set by this family. You can be full-time parents even if you both work.*

---

* Gene and Vicki Johnston have given their permission for me to use their example in this book.

Unit 5

Things That Destroy the Home

Children's Prayer Focus

Promise God that you will maintain a lifestyle of purity.

The seventh commandment, which we are studying this week, deals with more than just maintaining love for your marriage partner. The three-letter word "sex" has become a symbol for the abuse of the physical relationship God gave to two people for marriage.

God created sex as a gift to be used within marriage to strengthen the marriage relationship and allow a husband and wife to express their love for each other in an intimate and fully satisfying manner. Out of that expression of love the family would be birthed, and the opportunity for training a new generation for godliness would begin.

But Satan, who desperately wants to destroy the home, has taken this gift outside marriage and perverted it into one of the world's greatest sins. Adultery (which is sex with someone other than your marriage partner) and fornication (which is sex outside of marriage) have become acceptable.

How I wish we could prevent our children being exposed to the ugliness Satan has brought to this most intimate and tender act any of us may ever know. But it is nearly impossible to prevent our children's exposure to the devil's perversions.

The devil uses lust to draw people into sexual disobedience to God's laws. Lust is a desire for what is forbidden, a desire for things that are contrary to the will of God.

God has given us the power to resist lust through the help of the Holy Spirit. God wants us to be pure in thoughts and actions. The advice that Paul gave his young friend Timothy is advice that every young person should follow:

> *Flee also youthful lusts; but pursue right-eousness, faith, love, peace with those who call on the Lord out of a pure heart (2 Tim. 2:22).*

Make a commitment to purity now — while you are young.

(▶ Begin while your children are young to teach them the steps to making a lasting commitment to marriage. Build good communication with your children on the subject of their relationships, and pray together for the people God is preparing to bring into their lives as lifelong mates.

► Parent Tip

This page is for parents only. It is my hope that it will give both material and food for thought to help you teach this commandment to your children.

Your own life experiences may have dictated a course for your life and marriage that is different from the ideal God has given us to teach to our children. But God, who is infinitely more loving and wise than we can understand, will enable you to create a desire within the hearts of your children to exercise faithfulness to their own marriage vow when they come to that point in life. At the same time, He will give them a compassionate understanding for the pain that you have known.

During the dark days of World War II, family life as God intended it to be lived out began to break down in our nation. We are now faced with four decades of young couples who became biologically ready for marriage with little or no concept of what the marriage relationship should be like. Children learn by what is modeled before them.

Be comforted with the fact that God does not sit in judgment of our failed relationships. Be compelled with the transforming knowledge that God can enable us to bring our homes into His ideal. God will graciously bless our homes with security, stability and love — regardless of their makeup — as we commit to live and teach our children to live by His standards for the marriage relationship.

Week 13

Do Not Steal or Lie

Goal

To identify the motivations and actions that lead to stealing and lying.

Prayer Focus

Lead your family to identify impure, worldly motivations they may have allowed to creep into their lives. Ask God's forgiveness, and ask Him to help each family member grow spiritually.

▶ Spend some time alone with each of your children each day. These moments of intimacy are important opportunities for each child to clear his or her conscience. God gave us his "do not" commandments because He knew the effects of harboring sin in our hearts.

Unit 1

Where
Stealing Starts

Before we begin today, I want each one of you
to tell me what it means to steal. What is stealing?

Stealing starts in the heart. *All* sin starts in the
heart. Sin never just happens. We would like to
think it does, because that would let us off the
hook a lot easier, but that's not the way it is.

Stealing begins the same way every other sin
begins — with a flash of temptation. Then we
consider it in our mind and make the choice. During
that thought process, a "war" goes on inside as we
think about the law we will break if we choose to
do wrong.

The Bible tells us the story of Achan, a soldier
under Joshua, who disobeyed God's rule by
stealing a jeweled robe and a brick of gold from
the enemy during a battle. Because he knew he
was stealing, he hid the robe and gold in a hole

under the floor of his tent.

But sin cannot be hidden from God. God spoke to Joshua and said, "There is an accursed thing in your midst, O Israel; you cannot stand before your enemies until you take away the accursed thing from among you" (Josh. 7:13, KJV).

In order to find out which of his men had stolen something, Joshua lined them up by tribes to stand before him. The Lord spoke to Joshua and told him the thief was among the tribe of Judah. Then he lined up the tribe of Judah and God indicated the thief was among the clan of the Zarhites. When that clan stood before him, God earmarked the man Zabdi, then Zabdi's son Carmi, and finally the only man left was Carmi's son Achan. To Achan Joshua said,

> *My son, I beg you, give glory to the Lord God of Israel, and make confession to Him, and tell me now what you have done; do not hide it from me (7:19, KJV).*

When confronted with his sin, Achan confessed. Messengers went to Achan's tent, found the stolen items and brought them to Joshua. But Achan still had to face the consequences of his sin. Joshua took Achan to the valley where he told him: "Why have you troubled us? The Lord will trouble you this day."

And all the men of Israel stoned Achan to death.

Then they burned his body and buried him. Over his body they heaped a pile of stones that remained forever as a reminder of the consequences of Achan's sin of stealing. The valley was named Achor, which means "trouble."

Achan did not only have to die for his own sin — Israel lost the battle because of one dishonest man. When we are not right with God, we create problems for others.

We must be willing to stop our sinning and let Jesus change our lives. The book of Ephesians tells us: "Let him that stole steal no more: but rather let him labour, working with his hands the thing which is good, that he may have to give to him that needeth" (4:28, KJV).

DISCUSSION QUESTIONS

How do you think the sin of stealing began in Achan's heart?

Can you give an illustration of a time when someone thought they had hidden a sin, but God used circumstances to reveal their sin?

Has Satan ever tempted you to steal? How? What did you do about the temptation?

Unit 2

Is "That" Really Stealing?

Children's Prayer Focus

Ask God to help you recognize each subtle temptation.

Stealing is one of the things that everyone has to deal with because it is so subtle.

Many of us have taken a piece of candy when Mom wasn't looking. Or we may have grabbed a cookie off our sister's plate when she ran to answer the phone. Perhaps we failed to return the extra dollar the store clerk gave us at the checkout register.

We justify our actions by saying, "The candy belonged to our family. I didn't *steal* it!" "What's *one* cookie? My sister can get more if she wants to!" Or, "The clerk isn't going to miss one dollar!"

And it is true. None of those things were objects of great worth. But the problem rests in our heart.

Suppose you had decided, "God's law tells me to obey my parents. When Mom said, 'No candy before lunch!' that's the rule." You will feel wonderfully good about yourself. You have won a battle with the devil.

The smallest child *knows* when he or she takes something that belongs to another person. Satan tries to get us to hide our sin, but if we do we have allowed him to steal our joy.

One of the things that will help us to remember God's rules is to remember that God's presence is with us every moment of every day. He sees us when trouble threatens to destroy us and is quick to respond to our need. But he also sees us when we think no one else is watching — and knows the motives of our heart. He cheers us on with His, "Come on, child — you can serve Me; you can make the right decisions."

Get in the habit of picturing Jesus standing by your side. It will make it easier to defeat the devil's attempts to get you to be disobedient to His "do nots."

We must deal with temptation in our heart. We don't want you to ever let fear of discipline prevent you from keeping your hearts clean and happy.

One of the reasons we have a time alone with each of you at bedtime is so you can talk to us in privacy. Do not be afraid to share any truth about things you have done that were wrong. Satan wants to rob you of your happiness and security with your parents and with God. But we are here to help you become strong in obedience to God's rules. They will keep you from the guilt that would destroy you.

DISCUSSION QUESTIONS

What are some things that people often take, which actually may be stealing?

(▶ Be prepared to prompt for answers.)

How could each of the following be considered stealing?

1. Keeping the extra change the store clerk gives you by mistake.

2. Borrowing a pen from another classmate and then never returning it.

3. Eating the candy bar your sister left on the kitchen counter.

4. Copying, and claiming as yours, a "great" cartoon you found in a copyrighted magazine.

Unit 3

Michelle Confronts The Enemy

Let me tell you about Michelle. One day she was on the playground at her school, waiting to slide down the slide. There was a long line and she had only gone down the slide three times.

Standing about fourth in line was Kathy, a new girl in school. Knowing Kathy wanted to make friends with her, she said: "Kathy, can I take your turn? I'm not supposed to stay in the sun a long time without sunscreen! It won't take you very long to get back up here...would you mind?"

Kathy glanced at the line, then at Michelle's pleading face, and replied, "OK," and walked to the end of the line. But before she got a turn, the bell rang, ending recess.

Michelle had yielded to Satan's temptations to sin in several important areas.

First, Michelle failed to obey God's rule to treat

others as we want them to treat us. She would not want anyone to ask such a thing of her!

Earlier that morning, Michelle's mother asked if she had put on sunscreen, but Michelle had forgotten. "Michelle," her mom scolded, "you must become more responsible. At recess today, try to stay out of the sun as much as you can." So Michelle's second sin happened when she lied about why she needed Kathy's place. She had been instructed to stay out of the sun without sunscreen, but had been playing in the sun all during recess.

That night when Michelle's mom asked her if she had remembered to stay out of the sun, Michelle replied, "I sat at a table with the playground attendant until it was almost time to go in. Then I went down the slide just once!" Now we see her third sin — covering up her actions with a lie.

Finally, Michelle actually *stole* Kathy's turn, didn't she? And she dishonored her mother by not heeding her instructions.

Quite a few acts of disobedience occurred, didn't they? It is very easy to fall into these kinds of temptations and allow "little" sinful habits to form. Michelle is not that different from the rest of us. One sin leads to another, letting our heart grow darker and darker.

God will help us resist temptation. "The Lord knows how to deliver the godly out of temptations" (2 Pet. 2:9). He promises:

No temptation has overtaken you except such as is common to man; but God is faithful, who will not allow you to be tempted beyond what you are able, but with the temptation will also make the way of escape, that you may be able to bear it (1 Cor. 10:13).

Learn to look for the "way of escape" every time you are tempted.

DISCUSSION QUESTIONS

Has Satan ever drawn you into a series of disobedient actions as he did with Michelle? Describe the time.

Can you "rewrite" Michelle's story, giving us some better ways to respond to the methods the devil used to tempt Michelle?

Unit 4

Honesty With God

When we are honest with God, we grow closer and closer to Him. We allow Him to change the way we feel about sinful things.

If we are careless about the little habits of our heart, we will become less and less like Him and grow disinterested in the things He cares about. At those times, just as a Christian parent would discipline us, God will do the same. In kindness, God will allow trouble and heartache into our lives. It is His desire to wake us up to realize our lives are unpleasing to Him. He desires to shower us with blessings. But a holy God cannot bless a disobedient child.

Because we live in a world that belongs to the devil, it is far easier to grow cold in your heart, allowing it to become dark and hardened. Satan can make something look so right that it is hard for us to hear the still, small voice of God.

Knowing God's Word can help us avoid the snares of sin along life's path. The writer of Psalm 119 asked, "How can a young man cleanse his way?" (v.9). Then he answered the question by saying, "By taking heed according to Your word."

His example is worth following. He encourages us with these words:

> *With my whole heart I have sought You; oh, let me not wander from Your commandments! Your word I have hidden in my heart, that I might not sin against you...I will meditate on Your precepts, and contemplate Your ways. I will delight myself in Your statutes; I will not forget Your word (119:10-11, 15-16).*

Parents, grandparents, Christian teachers and leaders can help children to make the right choices. You can talk to us about your failures. Keeping them hidden within your heart would equal another failure — another wrong decision. Then the devil can tempt you even more. Have the courage to be open with the spiritual adults God has given to you so we can help you keep your heart open to God.

DISCUSSION QUESTIONS

Complete each of the following statements:

When I am unsure if something is the right thing to do, I can....

When I fail to do the right thing, it makes me feel better to talk about my failure with....

The Christians I look up to the most for direction and guidance are....

I want others to see Jesus living in my life the way I can see Jesus in the life of....

Unit 5

One Lie Leads To Another

Did you ever try to fool someone who was having a birthday party by topping his or her cake with those little candles that flame up again and again when you try to blow them out?

Lies are like that — they are hard to kill. They keep flaming up again and again as we try to cover up the last lie we told.

Maybe it happens something like this:

"Brian, how did you do on your test today?" Mom asks as you walk in the door after school.

"Oh, fine," you answer hurriedly, trying to avoid her "third-degree" questions.

"Well, what grade did you get?" she continues.

You know you flunked — the teacher told you that — but you say, "Oh, I think I got about a *C*." *(Lie #1)*

Mom drills you more: "Let me see your paper."

"Well, Miss Smith still has it." *(Lie #2)* You fail to tell your mother that it is really the wastebasket that has your paper.

When your mother asks to see it the next day, you say, "I forgot it. It's in my locker." *(Lie #3)* You hope she forgets about it too!

But she doesn't. "Brian, where's that test paper?" she asks on the third day.

Wanting to put an end to your misery, you answer, "Mom, you won't believe this, but I dropped it in a puddle, and the bus ran over it." *(Lie #4)*

By now Mom is on to you. "Bring me the phone. I want to call Miss Smith," she commands menacingly. Then one last try.

"But Miss Smith is at a seminar all weekend." *(Lie #5)*

The problem with lying is that it makes you a *liar*— a name none of us wants to have. Soon all your friends are saying: "Oh, forget anything Brian tells you! He wouldn't know the truth if it hit him over the head. He lies all the time!"

Break the power Satan has over you by getting you to lie. Say with the apostle Paul, "I speak the truth in Christ, and lie not" (1 Tim. 2:7).

DISCUSSION QUESTIONS

Can you think of an example of how one lie causes a person to cover up with another lie?

How can we break the power of lying that Satan tries to use to control us? (▶ Discuss James 4:7.)

What are some situations in which it would take a lot of courage to tell the truth?

What do the following verses tell us about lying?

- Psalm 52:3-5
- Psalm 119:29
- Proverbs 12:22
- Ephesians 4:25
- Revelation 21:8

Week 14

Do Not Want What Belongs to Others

Memory Verses

Psalm 23
Even though your children may know this Psalm, discuss it thoroughly with them this week. Be sure they can explain the chapter's meaning also.

Goal
To learn to use the tool of appreciation to defeat the devil's attack of covetousness.

Prayer Focus
Emphasize a different "goodness" of God from Psalm 23 each day:

- Monday — God supplies our need
- Tuesday — God supplies a place for us to live
- Wednesday — He gives us peace in our hearts
- Thursday — God gives us freedom from fear
- Friday — He guides us in our choices

Unit 1

But Everybody Has One

Covetousness is an intense desire to possess things we do not have, which usually are things we cannot afford. We take our eyes off the blessings God has given us when covetousness is given a place in our hearts.

An attitude of covetousness can creep into our hearts quickly. It makes you believe your discount store jeans are just not as nice as the ones with the designer label stitched on the pocket. Maybe your best friend has a brand new pair of Shaq basketball shoes, and all at once your Nike shoes look pretty shabby. Or you complain to your parents: "It's just not fair — *everybody else* got a new mountain bike for Christmas!"

We need to be able to be happy for our friends when they have something we would enjoy having. There might be a time when we will have the same things, but if it never happens, we still have a long list of wonderful things to be grateful for.

Jesus gave the illustration of a man who owned a vineyard (see Matt. 21:33-40). When he left on a journey, he trusted his workers to tend the vineyard for him and get it ready for harvest. But these men coveted the vineyard for themselves. When the man's servants went to the vineyard to pick up the fruit of the harvest, these wicked men killed them. They also killed the next group of servants that the landowner sent to get the harvest.

Finally the landowner sent his own son, believing, "They will respect my son" (v. 37).

But the wicked men said: "This is the heir. Come, let us kill him and seize his inheritance" (v. 38).

Covetousness must not be allowed in our lives. It is like a cancer that begins small but grows to gigantic proportions. Jesus said the best way to overcome a spirit of covetousness was to realize that "one's life does not consist in the abundance of the things he possesses" (Luke 12:15). It consists in a relationship with Christ.

If you know of anything you are unhappy about because you do not have it, we want so much for you to feel free to discuss it with us. You do not want your heart to get hardened because you have a secret you are fearful to share.

DISCUSSION QUESTIONS

Can you share a time when you had sudden, intense feelings of covetousness?

Can you name five things you do have for which you are very grateful?

How does covetousness find room in our hearts?

Unit 2

Jealousy and Envy

Children's Prayer Focus

Ask God to reveal any jealousy or envy hidden in your heart.

Jealousy and envy are two of the most miserable feelings in the world. God knew that when He gave us this tenth law. In this world, there is never going to be a time when someone else does not have something you would like to have.

There are some sins that are not things we do — they are things we think. Jealousy and envy are two of these sins. Jealousy makes us want to be the most important person in someone's life and causes us to resent any show of affection they give to another. Envy is the awful feeling we get inside about *things,* things that other people have and we don't have.

Jealousy and envy are often hidden in the heart. But, like other sins we have already discussed, these sins can affect the whole body. They shorten life, cause physical illnesses and destroy wonderful friendships. God does not want us to covet either by jealousy or envy, because He does not want us to experience such unhappiness.

Jenny was feeling sorry for herself because she had only two pairs of shoes. When her mother tried to explain why they could not afford a new pair of shoes, Jenny said: "I don't have anything nice. Kristen has a beautiful satin quilt on her bed, and all I have is this old quilt Granny made for me."

Her mother tried to tell her about the many hours Granny spent making that quilt just for Jenny, but she wouldn't listen. She began naming many more things she wished she had, never seeing the value of her own treasures.

The next time she visited Granny, she told Granny how she felt. Granny said, "Let's sit on the porch swing and have some lemonade." She carried out a tray with two glasses of lemonade — each only half full.

"Jenny," she asked, "are these glasses half full or half empty?"

Jenny thought a moment, and then replied, "Why...both!"

"That was all the lemonade I had," Granny continued. "Perhaps I should have filled your glass and gone without any myself."

"Oh, no," Jenny cried, "I would never want you to do that! I love to share with you, Granny."

Granny patted Jenny gently on the knee. "Most

families have to get along with glasses that are half full. For instance, in our family we always have good food on the table, warm beds to sleep in and clothes that are clean and presentable. But there are people who have more than we do — just like our half-full lemonade glasses. What matters is whether we choose to think about the half we have, or the half we don't have. Do we appreciate the half-full cup, or are we envious of those who have more?"

Jenny understood the message.

Let's keep our hearts thankful for what we have — not envious for what we lack.

DISCUSSION QUESTIONS

What lesson did Jenny learn about being envious of what others have?

How does being filled with envy for what you do not have make you feel?

Can you name some things that God has given to you for which you sometimes forget to thank Him?

Unit 3

Appreciation For What I Have

The best way to overcome the sin of covetousness is to develop an appreciation for the things that we do have.

Can each one of you think of some of the things you have for which you are grateful? Now, let's each thank the Lord for each of these things.

There will always be someone who has something nicer than you have. There will never come a time when you have everything that you want. But having something — or not having something — has nothing to do with your happiness. Happiness is more than the excitement of something new. It is peace of mind and contentment that everything is going well in your life. Happiness is knowing you have a clean heart.

We can be happy even in the midst of hard times. There will be times when we don't have enough money to do some of the things we'd like to do, but then we can stop and remember that we do have everything we need — and more.

One of the most important "things" to appreciate is our family! God has blessed us with people who love us and need our love in return. We need to think of ways daily to show how much we appreciate the unique contribution each family member makes to our happiness.

▓ The Hayford Heritage ▓

My husband and I experienced some difficult financial times during the years we were raising our young family. But God taught us a lesson we'll never forget, a lesson about trusting Him to provide for our needs.

When I began attending the little church where I was saved, I noticed a small box in the foyer marked with these words: "The Lord's Tithe." I noticed others putting money in it, so I just dropped whatever small change I was able to give into the box.

One night, two weeks after I was saved, I attended an evening service and went forward to the altar to pray at the end of the service. As I knelt, waiting my turn to be prayed for, I had a vision. It was a picture of a dime, hanging free as though it were blowing in the wind. The picture appeared to me three times.

Confused, I asked the pastor what it meant.

"Have you heard of the tithe?" he asked.

"No, but I know it has something to do with the money people put in that little box in the foyer," I replied.

In just a few minutes, the pastor explained the principle of the tithe in a way I could understand. Returning home, I told my husband what had happened.

"We can do that!" he told me when I finished. He took three cups down out of the cupboard. "A tenth of whatever we earn will go in this cup," he said, holding up the first cup. "Then we will divide the rest into the other two cups — half for rent and half for food."

It would be three years before my husband had a steady job. During that time, our needs, as well as our sensible, reasonable wants, were generously met. We often refer laughingly to those years as the "hand-to-mouth" years — God's hand to our mouths.

Unit 4

How to
Be Rich

The writer of Hebrews tells us:

*Let your conduct be without covetousness;
be content with such things as you have.
You are rich in the promise Jesus has
given you when He said, 'I will never
leave you nor forsake you.' (Heb. 13:5).*

The greatest wealth we could ever possess is
ours if we have Jesus in our hearts! There is nothing
we could own, no place we could go, no delicious
treat we could eat, that is worth anything at all
compared to the priceless treasure within our
hearts.

The Bible tells us the story of King Solomon, one
of the richest men that ever lived. His wealth is
described in 1 Kings 10:14-29. Yet all the riches that

Solomon possessed failed to satisfy the deepest longing of his soul. In his own words he states: "Vanity of vanities, all is vanity" (Eccl. 1:2). In fact, Solomon wrote the entire book of Ecclesiastes just to let us know that merely living our lives to satisfy our own covetousness and greed is pointless.

Solomon was not only one of the richest men to ever live — he was also one of the wisest, most accomplished and most successful people to ever live. And, perhaps, one of the most unhappy!

In the book of Ecclesiastes he lists the things he had attained that he found to be empty — just plain vanity. Some of these include:

- Human accomplishment
- Labor
- Money
- Material possessions
- Wisdom
- Power
- Strength
- Folly

▶ Spend some time discussing how each of the things listed above could fail to bring fulfillment to a person's life. Lead your children to see that while there is nothing wrong with any of the things on the list, not one of them is the one thing that will satisfy our hearts.

We can get a glimpse into Solomon's life by

looking at the eleventh chapter of 1 Kings. Right after the tenth chapter lists all the riches that Solomon possessed, we read: "*But* King Solomon loved many foreign women" (v.1).

Solomon coveted what he wasn't supposed to have. God had warned the Israelites, "Nor shall you make marriages with them [any of the nations which possessed the promised land before the Israelites]" (Deut. 7:3).

Coveting what we cannot have will keep us from becoming rich with what we can have — an exciting, intimate relationship with Jesus Christ.

It was Jesus Himself that instructed us: "Do not lay up for yourselves treasures on earth, where moth and rust destroy and where thieves break in and steal; but lay up for yourselves treasures in heaven, where neither moth nor rust destroys and where thieves do not break in and steal. For where your treasure is, there your heart will be also" (Matt. 6:19-21).

The only true and lasting riches are found in a life committed to Jesus Christ.

Unit 5

Be Content
With Your Life

In the New Testament, the apostle Paul is a good example of a man who learned to turn his desires from the things of earth to the things of heaven.

Even though Paul was a very religious Jew who kept all the commandments, he had not received Jesus into his heart. Like many of the religious leaders of his day, Paul adhered to God's rules because of the attention it brought to him, and for the position it gave him in the religious Jewish community.

Paul had taken a religious vow to serve God and await the coming of the Messiah. But when Jesus came, He was not what Paul and the religious leaders had expected. This man of lowly birth, who befriended sinners and healed on the Sabbath, did not appear to be a powerful leader who would take the nation back from the Romans.

Even after Jesus died, arose from the grave and proved to many that He was who He claimed to be, Paul still was determined to rid the nation of all Christ's followers.

Paul believed he was serving God with his actions. One day he began a journey that would change his life. While traveling to Damascus in pursuit of Christians, God literally knocked Paul off his horse and to the ground. As God revealed Himself to Paul, Paul realized his error and repented of his sin. At that moment he transferred his desires from things of earth to things of heaven.

Convinced of Jesus' love for all mankind, Paul renounced his own cause for the cause of Christ. He laid aside everything that had mattered to him — popularity, position, admiration and material possessions. These things he had coveted so much before meeting Christ on that road to Damascus now became a snare to avoid.

Paul learned to covet only his relationship to Christ. He never achieved great wealth or recognition among the Jewish leaders of his day. But he received the approval of God.

What was Paul's secret? It was, "I have learned in whatever state I am, to be content...I can do all things through Christ who strengthens me" (Phil. 4:11, 13). Learn to be content with what you have, desiring only to have Christ and His plan for your life.

DISCUSSION QUESTIONS

Describe the kind of man Paul was before he allowed Jesus to transform his life.

What were some of the worldly accomplishments and possessions that made Paul appear to be a very successful man?

What important lesson about his actions did Paul learn on the road to Damascus?

What evidence do we have that Paul learned to be content with his life after he met Jesus?

Week 15

The Family
Fruit Basket (Part 1)

Goal
To utilize the fruits of the Spirit to overcome the
sinful attitudes and behaviors within us.

Prayer Focus
During the times of daily prayer, focus on the fruit
being studied that day. Pray that it will be evident
in each person's life, and think of ways to show the
fruit to others.

▶ Use everyday anecdotes during the next two
weeks to help your children understand how the
fruit of the Spirit helps us to overcome problem attitudes or actions. Explain that we should each seek
to have these "fruits" ripening in our lives.

Unit 1

$\mathcal{S}eeds$ for
$\mathcal{T}he$ $\mathcal{F}uture$

In his book, *The Key to Everything*, Jack Hayford, our author's son, tells the story of John Chapman:

> *John worked in a western Pennsylvania
> cider mill...in the early 1800s...It was
> while he was working at the cider mill
> that John Chapman became possessed
> with an idea...that gripped his heart and
> became more influential in preparing the
> way for the future of a nation than he
> could ever have dreamed.*
>
> *One obvious by-product of work at the
> cider mill was...piles and piles of apple
> seeds, left over after the pressing process.
> One day...Chapman filled large bags with
> the seeds, quit his job and prepared to*

head west. As he traveled, he planted apple trees all along the way...He faced the elements, learning to interface with the Indians and meeting hardships in the pursuit of his dream.

Some...have said the man was insane...Others say the man was a pivotal personality in early U.S. history...They called him Johnny Appleseed.*

The apple seeds that Johnny Appleseed planted grew into fruit-bearing trees that provided sustenance and hope to many early settlers

Have you ever seen an apple tree with big, beautiful apples hanging from its branches? Fruit does not grow on the roots or the trunk of a tree. It doesn't even grow on the sturdiest of branches. There are smaller branches that grow out from the large limbs, and in the spring they are covered with bright new leaves. Then the tree produces glorious, brightly-colored blossoms. They are so beautiful we hate to see them go, but right in the heart of those blossoms is the beginning of the fruit that nourishes the hungry.

We are like the apple tree. We come to Jesus out of the cold winter of life without Him. Then His life begins to show like tender, new leaves. As His life fills ours, we blossom like the tree in His forgiveness and joy.

---

* Jack Hayford, *The Key to Everything* (Orlando, FL; Creation House, 1993), pp. 119-121.

Finally, the fruit of His presence begins to grow. The Bible describes this fruit as the "fruit of the Spirit." As we study the fruit of the Spirit for the next two weeks, we will discover that like oranges, apples and strawberries, spiritual fruit takes different lengths of time to become fully ripe. But as we allow His fruitfulness to develop in our lives, we will be transformed into His likeness. His fruit will grow out of our lives and affect the lives of many people around us.

DISCUSSION QUESTIONS

Thinking about the fruit mentioned, have each child relate which one they can see growing in each family member's life.

Which of the fruits of the Spirit do you think would be most helpful for you to develop in your own life?

Unit 2

To Be Like Jesus

Children's Prayer Focus

Thank God for the fruit of the Spirit, which will make you more like Jesus.

In the fifth chapter of Galatians, Paul compares the wicked practices of the unbeliever — the "fruit of the flesh" — to the new "fruit of the Spirit" that is produced in the life of the believer.

We can view the fruit of the Spirit by picturing a large fruit bowl, filled with nine different kinds of ripe, beautiful fruit. Our lives are like that fruit bowl, and within our lives the Holy Spirit is developing His fruit. The fruit is in different stages of development — not every fruit is fully evident. Like an orange tree, the choiceness of the fruit depends on how many years the tree has been bearing fruit. It takes time for fruit — natural or spiritual — to peak into full distinctive flavor.

When we receive Jesus into our lives, the Holy Spirit gives us a "jump start" of love, joy and peace. Can you remember the love you felt when you first came to Jesus? What a thrill to be loved by God. It was a wonderful feeling and people noticed a difference in our faces and in our behavior. We overflowed with the joy of knowing God's forgiveness and acceptance. We were suddenly at peace — all our guilt was gone.

We looked promising, but we were a long way from being ripe. It is appropriate that longsuffering comes next. Longsuffering is the willingness to patiently allow God to ripen us through obedience. It tags up with self-control to enable us to choose to do things the way Jesus wants us to do them.

At this stage of our growth, there may be a certain amount of inner irritation (suffering). It is commendable to do the right things because you want to be obedient, but Jesus wants His ways to become our own. However long it takes for us to suffer the death of our old selfish ways, He patiently gives us that time. He longs for us to bear fully-ripe fruit.

As we ripen further, we will exhibit fruits of kindness, goodness and faithfulness. We learn to behave in ways that cause happiness to those around us. We become dependable and trustworthy. We will not hurt people with our actions or words, but will be gentle and kind to others.

As we look closer at the nine fruits of the Spirit, ask God to help you find ways to let the fruit be evident in your daily life. Be the kind of "fruit bowl Christian" that is pleasing to God — be like Jesus!

DISCUSSION QUESTIONS

(▶ Look up the following scriptures and read them with the questions.)

What is happening when fruit is developing in our lives (Is. 28:9-10)?

Why does this take time (Phil. 3:21)?

Why is it important for us to be obedient to what we know of God's will (Deut. 5:29)?

Will we need to tell others we have "ripened fruit" in our lives?

Who do you know that exhibits the fruit of the Holy Spirit in their life?

Unit 3

The
Love Cloud

The fruit of love makes it hard not to let others
know you love them. It is filled with creativity and
affection, and reaches out from you to all the people
around you.

Our author describes an experience she had
with "the love cloud."

▓ The Hayford Heritage ▓

The most loving gift I ever received came
from my nine-year-old daughter. At Christmas
time that year, she visited a store where she
saw a little velvet tam with a beautiful scotch
plaid band that fit snugly to her head. Just
over her right eye, the tam had two beautiful
feathers complementing the colors of the tam.
There was a little velvet muff to match.

It was rather expensive, and not really

practical for warmth or durability. But her daddy believed that Christmas shouldn't be completely practical, so we purchased the set, wrapped it up and placed it under the Christmas tree.

Luanne loved it. She wore it every chance she had. When the weather warmed, she put it away carefully in a special box. She had never displayed such care for an article of clothing.

Just before Mother's Day she was promised a Saturday afternoon baby-sitting job with the two little children next door. She planned to use her earnings to buy a Mother's Day card and perhaps a small gift for me.

But the neighbor changed her mind about going out. Luanne was devastated. Her daddy offered her an advance on her allowance, but she didn't want to do that. She spent that Saturday afternoon up in her room. She loved to read, especially when she was discontented, and we assumed she was reading that afternoon.

The next morning was Mother's Day. I came down to the kitchen early in the morning to fix breakfast for the family. Sitting on the counter was a neatly wrapped little box. Luanne had taped a note to the box. On the note she had glued a cotton ball.

The note read: "This is a love cloud, blowing

love to my mother. The love it is bringing is inside the box."

I opened the box, and there on a little bed of cotton were the two feathers off her precious tam. No card or gift has ever meant more to me than that sacrificial love gift of my nine-year-old daughter.

DISCUSSION QUESTIONS

How did the fruit of love express itself in our author's story?

How has someone expressed the fruit of love to you?

Think of one person you are going to show love to, who will be surprised and happy by your attention.

Unit 4

Companion Fruit — Joy and Peace

Joy cannot be diminished. Sorrows may come. Difficulties may rob our hearts of outward peace. Happiness may seem to have disappeared. But when we think about the things that God has done for us, there is a joy and inner peace that floods our souls with just as much vigor as when we first experienced the joy and peace of salvation.

The Bible is filled with scriptures about the joy of the Lord. Joy is our strength (Neh. 8:10), it follows the darkness of sorrow (Ps. 30:5) and is our promised harvest (Ps. 126:5). As we allow the Holy Spirit to "ripen" our lives with His fruit, we will "go out with joy, and be led out with peace" (Is. 55:12). The final scripture reference to the fruit of joy is a benediction that promises:

Now to Him who is able to keep you from

stumbling, and to present you faultless before the presence of His glory with exceeding joy *(Jude 1:24).*

Like joy, peace is a gift beyond price. The peace that follows forgiveness of sin creates a haven within our soul. From that haven of safety and peace we move ahead in our lives with confidence, comfort and assurance even when we cannot see the end result. Such peace is like a green light — enabling us to become the people God created us to be.

It can also be a red light to our travel-weary souls. As our author sat at one red light after another on the way to her destination, she commented to her five-year-old grandson: "We're not having very good luck with these red lights, are we?"

Very philosophically he replied: "Gwamma, when we come to wed lights, we are apposed to west."

What great advice! When the red light is in my soul, I need to rest. And when the rest is restored through the fruit of peace and joy, I will undoubtedly be on my way.

The greatest joy of my life is the sight of my children, grandchildren and great-grandchildren gathered together, enjoying the simple pleasures of life. None of them is interested in pursuing the world's suggestions for having a good time.

They are bright, funny and gifted in so many different ways — writers, chemists and athletes. They are teachers, pastors, kids who are good scholars. There is no gift the world could give that would produce the joy and gratitude I experience when I am with my family, who are *all* with me in the Lord.

Unit 5

A Lesson In Longsuffering

God is the Grand Master of the fine art of long-suffering. Think what He has endured throughout the ages of the human race. Before He created us He knew the work it would take to conform us to His Son's image.

The fruit of longsuffering begins to develop when we receive Jesus as our Savior. But it requires a great deal of time and patience as God gently woos us to learn to choose His will for our lives.

Longsuffering comes as we learn to see others from God's point of view. That can only happen as we know His Word — both His written Word and His living Word, Jesus. Jesus is the perfect example of "full-fruited" godly living.

Jesus rejected no one. He was the friend of sinners. The only people he criticized were the religious leaders who rejected Him and His acceptance of others. Yet even these religious leaders would have received Jesus' full embrace and acceptance if they had chosen to turn their lives over to God.

There is no sin too heinous to be forgiven, no behavior too odious to disqualify a person from coming to Christ in confession and repentance. He sees beyond that person's actions and despises only the devil, His archenemy, who bent and twisted the person's life with sin.

We need to follow Christ's example of longsuffering. (▶ Ask the children to name someone who is difficult to enjoy. How does God see that person? How would Christ relate to him or her?)

If you have responded to that person with less than love and acceptance, admit your wrong to God.

Criticism about someone else's flaws is a shortcoming in your own life.

Learn to look at others as small infants who are just learning to walk. Or as people who have been handicapped by debilitating accidents. Pray for them, and believe for God to provide healing for them through the mercy and grace of Jesus. God knows how to reach into each person's life and restore spiritual health and wholeness if someone cares enough to pray.

It will amaze you to discover how much the fruit of longsuffering can be developed in your own life by such acceptance of others.

Longsuffering — it looks like patience in me; it feels like acceptance to another; and it keeps me aware of the process of becoming Christlike — like the Lord, who is so longsuffering with me.

DISCUSSION QUESTIONS

How has God exhibited longsuffering in His relationship with mankind?

Think of an instance where Jesus is a perfect example of "full-fruited" godly living.

Give an example of a time when you "suffered long" because of abusive treatment by another person. Did you try to find ways to treat that person as Christ would have treated him or her?

In what areas of your life do you believe you still need to develop more longsuffering?

Week 16

The Family
Fruit Basket (Part 2)

Memory Verse

*But the fruit of the Spirit is love, joy,
peace, longsuffering, kindness, goodness,
faithfulness, gentleness, self-control.
Against such there is no law.*

Galatians 5:22-23

Goal
To continue learning to use the fruit of the Spirit to
overcome sin.

▶ Display several kinds of fruit, purposely selecting
fruit that is in top edible condition, but not the
"cream of the crop" demanding top dollar. God is
not looking at the outward person — He is interested in what is on the inside. People don't run
around telling how mature they are in certain
ways. They just demonstrate it in their lives. A
peach may have a couple of spots on it where a
bird "nipped it," or a slight bruise where you
dropped it on the drain board, but it will still make
a great pie.

Unit 1

Kindness and Goodness Go Hand In Hand

Children's Prayer Focus

Ask God for opportunities to show kindness and goodness to family and friends.

The Bible speaks about God's lovingkindness. We are going to look at some scriptures to find ways to show the fruit of kindness. Some suggestions from this unit may be helpful, but there are many more creative ways to be kind and good.

1. God's lovingkindness overcomes the effect of war.

> *Show Your marvelous lovingkindness by Your right hand, O You who save those who trust in You from those who rise up against them (Ps. 17:7).*

Our world is not filled with kind, good people. There are children around the world who have not experienced kindness or goodness in a very long time. Pray for the children of other countries whose parents are fighting in wars and uprisings. Pray for God's protection from the ravages of war.

2. God's lovingkindness overcomes bad habits and behavior.

> *Do not withhold Your tender mercies from me, O Lord; let Your lovingkindness and Your truth continually preserve me (Ps. 40:11).*

To preserve something means "to keep it from spoiling." This verse is a good prayer for someone who is learning to be victorious over a bad habit or behavior. God will keep us from being spoiled by sinful habits and attitudes.

3. God's lovingkindness helps us learn to worship God with our praise.

> *We have thought, O God, on Your lovingkindness, in the midst of Your temple (Ps. 48:9).*

Think about the choruses and praise songs your church sings during worship times. These are words of appreciation for God's goodness to us. Sing these words with sincerity. When you go to church, remember you are visiting God's house. It can be an awesome time of meeting with God and experiencing His kindness and goodness.

4. God's lovingkindness reaches out to me with forgiveness.

> *Have mercy upon me, O God, according to your lovingkindness; according to the multitude of Your tender mercies, blot out my transgressions (Ps. 51:1).*

How wonderful to realize that God has blotted out our failure and sin. Pray this scripture prayer when you confess your sins to God. It will fill you with love, joy and peace as you experience God's great mercy and forgiveness.

Remember that God's example of kindness and goodness to us is one we are to follow in our actions to others. Ask God to lead you into specific opportunities to express kindness and goodness to the people around you. You will be a fruit-grower each time you do.

Unit 2

The Fruit
Of Faithfulness

Children's Prayer Focus

*Thank God for the opportunity
to be His faithful servant.*

Being faithful is not just something you *do* — it is something you *are!*

A speaker once gave this illustration. God wants us to be His hand. He is the Head. Until He calls upon us to do something, He would appreciate His hand being at rest, trusting that He will let it know when there is opportunity to serve.

How would you feel if you were awakened one morning by your hand tapping you on the head and calling, "O wonderful head, here I am! I have come to serve you. I know of so many things that need to be done around here. I am going to get busy and bless you, O head!" Then your hand runs off to do his "good works."

Meanwhile, your head wags from side to side, thinking, Bless my well-intended little hand. I wonder when it will mature sufficiently to *just wait* until *I* give it a job to do?

Faithfulness is availability — trustworthiness to "be there" when it counts. It is like the loving servant who sits at the feet of his master, ready and willing to do whatever the master requires of him. But he waits for the master's command, quietly, patiently and unobtrusively.

God's faithfulness should be so deeply reflected in the lives of His people that they can be called simply "the faithful" (Ps. 31:23). The greatest praise we will ever hear are the words with which we long to be greeted at heaven's gates:

> *Well done, good and faithful servant...*
> *Enter into the joy of your Lord (Matt.*
> *25:23).*

DISCUSSION QUESTIONS

How did the illustration of the hand of God describe faithfulness?

Tell of someone you believe has demonstrated great faithfulness in their actions.

How could the following people show great faithfulness by their actions?

- A Sunday school teacher

- A Christian Little League player who almost never gets to play

- A young girl who is asked to baby-sit for her younger brother every day after school

- A teenage boy who plays the piano for his church's youth ministry

- A father who loves to play golf on Saturday, but has a son in a Saturday soccer league

Unit 3

Gentle
Fruit Living

The tiniest children understand gentleness.

- "Just kiss him on his cheek. We have to be very gentle with the baby!"
- "Pick the kitten up very carefully. Kitties can be hurt if we do not handle them gently."
- "Don't be afraid, honey. Our dentist is a very gentle man."

If you heard these statements spoken aloud, you would notice that even the tone of voice is altered when we are speaking of gentleness.

Gentleness is caring. It understands that everyone is different. Gentleness takes the time needed to know how to be gentle at every turn.

Gentleness has nothing to do with strength or weakness. It is an attitude, a predisposition to acting in such a way as to treat another person with just exactly the treatment they need — and deserve from us.

The apostle Paul pleaded with us to be gentle with all people: "Let your gentleness be known to all men" (Phil. 4:5).

The Bible continues by giving us some examples of times when we are to express this fruit of gentleness.

> *But we were gentle among you, just as a nursing mother cherishes her own children (1 Thess. 2:7).*

We are to be gentle with anyone who needs our nurturing and care.

> *And a servant of the Lord must not quarrel but be gentle to all, able to teach, patient, in humility correcting those who are in opposition (2 Tim. 2:24-25)*

We must be gentle with those who oppose us, or with whom we find ourselves in the midst of an argument. Even when we are right, we are to teach them and correct them in a gentle manner.

> *But the wisdom that is from above is first pure, then peaceable, gentle, willing to yield, full of mercy and good fruits (Jas. 3:17).*

Even when we are in a position of importance or stature, still we are to be gentle with those who are under us, not trying to appear to be someone great and unapproachable but someone to whom anyone may come into fellowship with.

Gentleness must be a way of life for the believer. The fruit of gentleness should be evident in every action we take, with every word we speak and to every person we meet.

DISCUSSION QUESTIONS

Can you give an example of a way someone showed gentleness to you or in a situation you observed?

How could you show gentleness:

- to someone who needs your care?

- to a person who is arguing with you, even though you know you are right?

- to your students, if you were an eighth-grade math teacher?

Unit 4

Add the Fruit
Of Self-Control

The last of the nine fruits of the Spirit is the fruit
of self-control. Perhaps it is listed last for this reason:
Parts of each of the other eight fruits are needed to
develop fully the fruit of self-control.

If I do not have love in my heart for God and a
Jesus kind of love for other people, I may say or
do hurtful and mean things. It is difficult for me to
control my actions without love. Jesus must teach
me how to act as He acted in tough situations.

I can only feel good about myself when I am
obedient to what my parents and God's laws tell
me to be and do. When I do control my actions,
bringing them into obedience, my life is filled with
joy.

As I recognize the irritating things that someone
else is doing as brokenness instead of meanness, I
find that I am willing to suffer long to give that person

opportunity to change. My self-control helps me to allow them the freedom to become what God wants them to be.

The love chapter (1 Corinthians 13) speaks of a number of kind, good and gentle attitudes that enable the believer to be self-controlled. These are qualities that we are best able to recognize in others when we have demanded them of ourselves. The fruit of self-control develops as a result of allowing the fruits of kindness, goodness and gentleness to develop in our lives first.

A life that exhibits self-control is a life with inner peace. It is a life that is lived in faithfulness and loyalty to God and others. It has fully ripened to the point of fruit-bearing, and it offers to all who come in contact with it a beautiful, varied, "nine-fruit" medley of spiritual "fruit-living."

Self-control is no longer a problem, for Jesus is truly in control of such a life:

> *Suffers long and is kind; love does not envy, love does not parade itself, is not puffed up; does not behave rudely, does not seek its own, is not provoked, thinks no evil; does not rejoice in iniquity, but rejoices in the truth; bears all things, believes all things, hopes all things, endures all things. Love never fails (1 Cor. 13:4-8).*

DISCUSSION QUESTIONS

Why did our author believe God left the fruit of self-control as the last in our study?

How are each of the other eight fruits used to help us learn self-control?

- love
- joy
- peace
- longsuffering
- kindness
- goodness
- faithfulness
- gentleness

Unit 5

Upset the Fruit Basket

For the last two weeks we have been studying about the different fruits of the Spirit. By now you can see how important it is that we develop these fruits in our own lives.

These fruits can be used to overcome the works of the flesh that are mentioned in Galatians 5:19-21. In fact, they can be used to overcome any temptation that Satan hurls our way.

Let's play "Fruit of the Spirit Charades." Our game is played by teams. One family member will act out the negative sinful attitude while we try to guess it. Then the one who guesses correctly will get to act out the corresponding positive fruit of the Spirit. Let's see if we can guess all nine fruits.

▶ Follow the directions on the following page.

Fruit of the Spirit Charades

The negative attitudes and corresponding fruits are shown on the following page. Write each negative attitude with its corresponding fruit on a slip of paper.

Suggest that family members act out an example of the positive fruit that can be used to overcome a negative attitude. Be ready to help with an example where it is needed.

Choose one family member to act out the first positive fruit of the Spirit. When someone guesses the fruit correctly, allow that person to read the negative attitude that fruit overcomes. Discuss situations where this negative attitude could be corrected by using the corresponding fruit of the Spirit. Continue until you have completed all nine fruit.

Be sure each family member is allowed to act out at least one charade.

Discuss the fruit, asking for illustrations of times when each fruit of the Spirit could be used to change a negative temptation into a positive experience, with God's help.

Fruit of the Spirit Charades

NEGATIVE ATTITUDE	POSITIVE FRUIT
☹ Hatred and/or Murder	☺ Love
☹ Discouragement and/or Depression	☺ Joy
☹ Arguments and Chaos	☺ Peace
☹ Selfishness and/or Impatience	☺ Longsuffering
☹ Mean, Uncaring Actions	☺ Kindness
☹ Disobedience	☺ Goodness
☹ Disloyalty	☺ Faithfulness
☹ Abusive Actions	☺ Gentleness
☹ Anger	☺ Self-Control

What Has God Given You?

Memory Verse

Having then gifts differing according to the grace that is given to us, let us use them: if prophecy, let us prophesy in proportion to our faith; or ministry, let us use it in our ministering; he who teaches, in teaching; he who exhorts, in exhortation; he who gives, with liberality, he who leads, with diligence; he who shows mercy, with cheerfulness.

Romans 12:6-8

Goal

To recognize that God has gifted each family member with specific spiritual abilities.

Prayer Focus

Use the prayer time this week to focus on the unique gifts and abilities God has given to individual family members. Help your children to recognize their gifts. Lead them to discover ways to use these gifts while they are young. Guide them to understand their potential for future ministry.

Unit 1

What Can I Give Him — Child That I Am?

Children's Prayer Focus

Ask God to reveal the special gifts and abilities you have to give to Him.

I would like to excite you with a great possibility: You can give God the gift He desires above all others — obedience!

Obedience is such a common word but such an uncommon practice. Probably not a day passes for any of us without an awareness that we have "messed up" in at least one area of obedience.

The reason God hates sin so much is because it takes up room in our lives that He wants to fill with His ways and His blessings. But as we learn to live in obedience, God gifts each one of us with special abilities and blessings. He wants us to recognize these gifts and commit them to His service.

During this final week of our study in this book, we will take a look at some of these gifts and abilities. You may discover that God has given you just a "seed" of one or more of these. But as you live your life in obedience to His plan for you, these seeds will sprout up into opportunities for service.

Our memory verse lists seven spiritual gifts. They are:

- Prophecy
- Ministry
- Teaching
- Exhortation
- Giving
- Leading
- Mercy

Each of these spiritual gifts is available to each of us. These gifts were evident in the life of Christ, and as we become more and more Christlike, they will be more and more evident in our lives.

A little African American boy stood on a busy street corner, watching a street vendor selling brightly colored balloons. Every so often the vendor would release one of the helium-filled balloons. The little boy watched while first a red balloon, then a green and finally a white balloon sailed up into the clouds above.

Finally he could stand it no longer. He walked over to the vendor, tugged on his sleeve and asked, "Mister, if you let go of a black balloon, will it go up too?"

Perhaps this little boy had experienced a form of

prejudice that taught him black does not "go up."

But the wise, old street vendor looked down at the little boy's face. Kneeling down beside him, the vendor replied, "Son, it's what's inside these balloons that makes them go up!"

It's what's inside us that makes us "go up" to become all that God created us to be. He has saved us, filled us with the Holy Spirit and transformed our lives into the image of His own Son, Jesus. He has given us His rules to live by and promised us that if we are obedient to His ways, He will develop the fruit of the Spirit in our lives. He gifts us with spiritual blessings and abilities. We will live successful spiritual lives if we simply follow His plan for our lives.

DISCUSSION QUESTIONS

Which of the spiritual gifts mentioned in today's unit do you believe you may possess in "seed" form?

Can you name some ways that you can begin to use the spiritual gifts God has given to you?

Which gift do you think is most evident in your life?

Unit 2

The Gifts of Prophecy and Ministry

Children's Prayer Focus

Ask God to help you use His Word to help other people.

When you were born, more than a new baby came into our home. Little signs were evident from the start that God had put spiritual qualities within you that would be of tremendous help to you when they were fully developed.

Prophecy is one of these spiritual gifts. The word "prophesy" means "to speak for the Lord." It also means "to preach God's Word." However, it has an even broader meaning. If Jesus lives within our lives, we should be living in such a way that our lives are a "sermon."

Some of us will never stand on a podium and preach a "real" sermon. But our lives should prophesy, or tell forth, what our hearts believe. God asked each believer to let others know He loves them. Some of us are more gifted at this than others are.

The gift of prophecy gives us a boldness to speak in an appealing way to others about God. It "graces" us with an anointing that causes our words to be good news to the one who hears us. If God gives this gift to you, use it to be the best "delivery boy" for God that you can be.

Most of us will never occupy positions that make our name known to multitudes of people. God has need of such people, but their rewards will be no greater than the rewards He gives to us if we are faithful to the little behind-the-scenes tasks He sets before most of us.

In a family there will always be some who just naturally help or serve the other family members without giving a lot of thought to what they are doing. That is the gift of ministry.

If you are a helper — a person who loves to help, doing it cheerfully and without an expectation of praise or reward — you probably have the gift of ministry. Praise God for this gift; it takes you one step closer to our goal of Christlikeness.

DISCUSSION QUESTIONS

Can you give an example of a time when the gift of prophecy could be used?

When did you have an opportunity to "tell forth" some news about Jesus to another person?

What is the gift of ministry?

How does the gift of ministry move us closer to the goal of becoming Christlike in our actions and attitudes?

Unit 3

Gifts of Teaching, Exhortation and Leading

Children's Prayer Focus

*Ask God to help you teach
others about Christ.*

From the beginning of time, God has gifted some people with particular skills to teach people. Often the people chosen to help these teachers are individuals with a desire to learn the skill or knowledge that the teacher possessed.

Before there were formal schools, vocational skills were learned through an apprenticeship. A person skilled in a chosen vocation was given oversight of a young person's life while that young person learned the skill. Today we have teachers whose job it is to train others in a particular skill or knowledge.

Parents have been given the job of training children to know God's rules. Sunday school teachers teach God's Word, and professors train young people to serve the Lord in full-time ministry.

Perhaps some of you will be teachers. That ability

will be evident early in your life. You may be able to help someone understand a homework assignment or to teach a smaller child to make a bed properly.

The gift of exhortation can be defined as "calling near, entreating, warning or pleading." Many evangelists and pastors possess this gift, as evidenced by their compelling, life-changing messages from God's Word.

Jesus used this gift effectively as He called people into a lifelong relationship with God. He exhorted lovingly and intimately, weeping over the city of Jerusalem and pausing to call Zacchaeus out of a tree so He could share God's love with him.

He did not call down the wrath of God on those to whom He spoke. He demonstrated the gifts of teaching and exhortation in love. We should do the same. However, the best teacher in the world cannot succeed with a person who does not want to learn.

My husband and I believed that we had to be committed and imaginative with our Bible teaching in order to keep a single Bible truth alive and fresh for several days while our children digested it thoroughly. We knew that we had been successful when our children began to live out the principles in their lives.

One summer our son Jack's youngest child was with us while his parents were holding seminars in several churches. My husband had been teaching the children the story of "the Redeemer, the Receiver and the Rejecter." He had enlisted the children's help to tell the story from night to night.

One night the traveling parents stopped by. "Well, Jack," our son asked his preschool-age son, Jack. "What have you learned at Grandpa's house?"

To our amazement and pleasure little Jack launched right in, telling the story with great enthusiasm and accuracy.

Even very small kids can grasp Bible truths and remember them vividly. Jack was able to tell the story because we had reviewed and rehashed it with him three or four times the week before.

Unit 4

𝒯𝒽𝑒 𝒢𝒾𝒻𝓉
𝒯𝒽𝒶𝓉 𝒢𝒾𝓋𝑒𝓈

Children's Prayer Focus

*Thank God for giving you so
many blessings.*

God has a great big giving heart. He patiently endures the sins of mankind while He waits for the fruit of His giving to appear. He tenderly cares for His children who are slowly developing "according to His plan."

He has given life and forgiveness freely. He gave His own Son as a ransom for our sins. He gave the Holy Spirit to teach us how to be transformed into Christlikeness.

He gave a world filled with the beauty of His own creativity. He gifted us with spiritual fruits and gifts. He waits to give us His final gift — an eternity in His presence.

He *commands* us to give to Him. The Israelites were exhorted to bring their tithes into the store-house in order to enjoy God's blessing (Mal. 3:8-12). But His command was given with a promise:

'And try Me now in this,' says the Lord of hosts, 'If I will not open for you the windows of heaven and pour out for you such blessing that there will not be room enough to receive it.'

God does not command us to give only our money. He has demonstrated many different ways to give. We are to know His Word and recognize the opportunities we have to give. We are to give Him our time, talents, service, skills, possessions — we are to give Him everything.

He promises that our obedience will bring us a miraculous return. He will give back to us so that we can turn around and give Him more.

We can never outgive God. The more we give to Him, the more He returns to us. That return should never be our motivation — but it is our reward.

Give, and it will be given to you: good measure, pressed down, shaken together, and running over will be put into your bosom. For with the same measure that you use, it will be measured back to you (Luke 6:38).

DISCUSSION QUESTIONS

The greatest example of the gift of giving is God Himself. Name some of the ways in which God has shown the gift of giving to you.

Malachi 3:8-12 promises that God will pour out blessings to us if we give to Him. What blessings has God poured into your life as a result of your obedience to give to Him?

What do you think Luke 6:38 means when it states: "For with the same measure that you use, it will be measured back to you"?

Unit 5

Use Mercy Prayerfully

Children's Prayer Focus

Thank God for the mercy He shows to us every day.

Mercy! What a wonderful gift. Where would we be without the mercy of God? Mercy lets us start over when we make the wrong move in a game. Mercy prompts us when we don't know the answer to a question. Mercy puts her arm around you when you are afraid of the darkness.

If you are inclined to feel sorry for the underdog, you are probably a "mercy person." But you will have to protect this gift to ensure that you do no harm with it.

Let me tell you about Tanya. One day Tanya was walking home from school with a friend who was a diabetic and therefore not supposed to eat any candy. Tanya spotted a five-dollar bill in the gutter. She picked it up and squealed: "I'm going to spend this *whole* thing on candy! I have never in my entire life had all the candy I wanted."

Meredith, the friend walking with her, frowned and said, "I can't eat any of it!"

Tanya thought for a minute. "Well," she replied, "I can't eat it all in one day. I'm going to hide it and make it last a long time. If you only ate one piece every day, I don't think that would hurt anything."

Meredith became excited at the thought. "You know what?" she whispered to Tanya. "Don't *ever* tell anyone, but sometimes I sneak a piece of candy when no one knows, and I don't get really sick. It just changes my blood sugar a little. It goes away the next day. I'll hide my candy too."

They ran all the way to the candy store and spent almost twenty minutes picking out their pieces of candy. Then they headed home. It was Friday, so they wouldn't see each other for several days.

Tanya's mother met her at the door when she returned from school on Monday. "Tanya, have you been keeping a secret — like perhaps finding some money?"

Tanya was not used to doing the kind of thing she had done, and broke into tears. "Oh, mamma," she said. "I've been so miserable. I spent it all on candy, and I haven't liked it a bit."

Mother took Tanya's chin in her hand. "And you gave half to Meredith?"

"Yes, but...."

"Meredith's mother just phoned me from the hospital. Meredith is very, very sick from all the candy she says you gave to her!" Tanya's mother went on to tell her that Meredith had eaten her whole bag of candy during that weekend.

Tanya felt terrible. She was shaken because her deception had been discovered. She felt awful because she suggested that Meredith hide some of the candy. But most of all, she was deeply frightened about Meredith's physical condition. She had missed Meredith at school that day, but she had not thought about the candy at all.

"But, Mamma," Tanya blurted out. "I felt so sorry for her because she can't eat any candy at all. At least she isn't supposed to."

"Tanya," her mother said. "We have talked many times about how thankful we are that you are so sympathetic to everyone's problems. But we have also warned you to consider the whole picture. Mercy can do damage as surely as it can do good. This is something you must learn once and for all."

Remember, if you are a "mercy person," be sure you are doing the right thing when you feel sorry for someone. You may be a party to something that is not right.

Week 18

Learning To Serve

Goal
To plant a desire within each family member to know and follow God's direction for his or her life.

Prayer Focus
During this final week of study in this book, pray that God will direct your family into the kind of continuing study He knows is best for your family. Perhaps you will want to continue with another devotional guide. Or you may want to develop your own family study based on the particular spiritual needs within your own family. Consider the suggestion of familiarizing your children with the entire Bible, its sections and their stories.

Unit 1

How Do I Do God's Will?

Children's Prayer Focus

Pray for an understanding of God's will for your life.

Micah tells us three things that are God's will for every person: "He has shown you, O man, what is good; and what does the Lord require of you but to do justly, to love mercy, and to walk humbly with your God?" (Mic. 6:8).

The word just means "fair." God wants our actions to be fair to those around us. He wants us to love showing mercy to others. By being merciful to others, we can demonstrate how to walk humbly with our God

"You broke my bike. You're going to pay for it out of your own money, girl. I'm never going to let you ride my bike again — *ever!*"

Those were the words of Amy, who had just received a new bike for her birthday. Dad had wheeled it out front for her, and she rode it three times around the block.

Then, at Dad's suggestion, she allowed her younger sister, Lisa, to take a turn. After going around the block, Lisa hopped off the bike and started to lower the kickstand. It broke off when she pushed it down and the bike crashed to the ground, denting the rear fender.

We can all sympathize with Amy. Her brand new bike was broken before it had even been put away once! But think about how Lisa must have felt. Not only was she frightened about what had happened, she was upset by her sister's wrath. She was fearful that she had done something wrong to cause the accident.

Holding her hands over her ears, she tried to scream above her sister's accusations: "I'm sorry, I'm sorry! I don't know how I did it, but I'm really sorry!"

Mom, hearing the tumult, came running. She thought one of the girls had been seriously hurt. When she noticed the absence of blood, she took each girl firmly by the shoulder and said quietly, "Let's sit down and talk about this."

Quiet descended upon the scene — but not upon Amy's spirit.

Dad joined the scene and inspected the bike. While Mom waited for Dad's report, she asked, "Amy, do you really believe that Lisa purposely broke the kickstand on your bike?"

Although she was still seething inside, Amy knew she had better answer carefully. "Well...no, she probably didn't *mean* to," she began.

By this time Dad had discovered a flaw in the metal kickstand. The accident would have occurred no matter who put down the kickstand.

Sitting down beside the two girls, he asked, "Do you know the worst thing that happened here?"

Both girls shook their heads.

Dad continued: "The worst thing is your behavior, Amy. I understand how disappointed you are. But I can take the bike back. It had a faulty part. But before I get the bike fixed, I want to fix my girls. God has instructed His people to love mercy. That is the will of God for our family. Even if Lisa had caused the kickstand to break, would she have done it on purpose?"

Both girls were crying now, and Amy tried one more time. "But, Daddy, it's so new!"

Her father took hold of her chin and looked into her eyes. "How would you feel, Amy, if the bike had been given to Lisa and *you* had the accident?"

That did it! Turning to Lisa, Amy apologized. Suddenly Lisa began to giggle. "This is like the poster we just hung up in our bedroom! I needed mercy — and you are giving it to me lovingly!"

Mom smiled and said, "I am proud of you girls. You are demonstrating how to please God and do His will. You are the picture of mercy. And you are now 'walking humbly with your God.'"

Unit 2

God's Great Promises

One of the greatest promises God made to His people says: "Now this is the confidence that we have in Him, that if we ask anything according to His will, He hears us. And if we know that He hears us, whatever we ask, we know that we have the petitions that we have asked of Him" (1 John 5:14-15).

This promise tells us that if we ask God for things according to His will, He will answer our prayers.

But how can we know if the things we are praying about are "according to His will"? If we have allowed Jesus to live in our lives, and listened to the voice of the Holy Spirit deep within, we will instinctively *know* if we are asking God for the right things most of the time. Our desires will be His desires, and His Son who lives within us will conform our wills to His own will.

God gave another great promise in the twenty-eighth chapter of Deuteronomy: "Now it shall come to pass, if you diligently obey the voice of the Lord your God, to observe carefully all His commandments which I command you today, that the Lord your God will set you high above all nations of the earth. And all these blessings shall come upon you and overtake you, because you obey the Lord your God" (vv. 1-2).

God wants to pour His love and goodness on His children. If we do our part, He will do His! Our part is to obey Him diligently and to carefully observe all His commandments. His part is to cause His blessings to "come upon" us and to "overtake" us.

God's blessings are much like a flash flood that chases after a tiny rowboat, overtaking it and flooding it with water. But God's blessings are for our benefit — not our destruction.

God is a good and faithful Father to His children. His will is meant to bless our lives. He will take care of His children and reveal Himself in many different ways to those who do their part and obey His commandments. Choose God's will; let His blessings overtake your life as you live in obedience to His commandments.

DISCUSSION QUESTIONS

How can we be sure we are praying for the right things?

What part must we perform if we are to receive the blessings of God for our lives?

Can you give an example of a time when you chose to obey God, thus receiving a blessing from Him?

Can you name some of the blessings God has for His children?

Unit 3

A Proof
Of Our Love

Children's Prayer Focus

*Express to God an action you will take
to prove your love for Him.*

(▶ This would be a good time to consider your next project. I would suggest learning the books of the Bible, along with the divisions in each of the testaments — law, history and so forth. Take a week on each segment, zeroing in on one story in that segment.)

Our decision to study God's Word together as a family was a way to prove our love for God. Every commandment God gives — whether it is something to do or something not to do — is an expression of His will for us.

Obedience is the highest gift of love we can offer to God. It was the highest gift of love that Jesus offered to His Father — God. He said, "I have come...to do Your will, O God" (Heb. 10:7).

Jesus' gift of obedience was costly to Him. Hebrews also tells us, "Who for the joy that was set before Him endured the cross, despising the shame" (12:2). He proved His love for God by obediently dying for our sin, even though it was a terrible, shameful death — which in no way Jesus deserved.

Paul speaks about knowing Jesus in the "fellowship of His suffering" (Phil. 3:10). This is not really hard to understand. For children, it means doing what is right even if people make fun of you for doing it. We prove our love by being obedient — even if we suffer the disapproval of others.

Paul often experienced the disapproval of others as he sought to do God's will. Yet he wrote:

> *Therefore I take pleasure in infirmities; in reproaches, in needs, in persecutions, in distresses; for Christ's sake. For when I am weak, then I am strong (2 Cor. 12:10).*

Paul experienced, just as Jesus experienced, the joy that comes to us because of our obedience. Psalm 119:2 tells us, "Blessed are those who keep His testimonies, who walk in the law of the Lord!"

Doing God's will no matter what we suffer is a proof of our love for Him. And receiving His blessings is greater than anything we could receive from people on earth.

There are hundreds of different ways in which God will bless His children. I want to be His obedient child — don't you?

DISCUSSION QUESTIONS

How can we prove our love for God?

Why is obedience the highest gift of love that we can offer to God?

▶ Spend some time discussing blessings that members of your family have received from God because they made hard decisions to do what was right.

Take the time to lay hands on each of your children and pray that God will give each child a loving, obedient heart.

Unit 4

A New Commandment

Children's Prayer Focus

*Ask God to help you fulfill His New
Testament commandments.*

Although we no longer have to go through the rituals of sacrifice as Old Testament people had to do, we must still be obedient to the commandments of God.

During the time Jesus lived on earth, some of the religious leaders had developed their own laws about how the people should live. Many of these laws had nothing to do with God's Word. Jesus spent much of His time on earth trying to teach the people correctly. But this often caused trouble with the religious leaders who claimed that Jesus was not keeping the Law.

One day they thought they had figured out a way to snare Jesus and prove His deception. They confronted Him with the question, "Which is the greatest commandment in the law?" (Matt. 22:36).

Jesus was ready for their attack and responded

with two New Testament commandments. He said, "You shall love the Lord your God with all your heart, with all your soul, and with all your mind. This is the first and great commandment. And the second is like it: You shall love your neighbor as yourself. On these two commandments hang all the Law and the Prophets" (vv. 37-40).

Jesus felt strongly about how we should treat one another. So should we! Family members should treat one another with love and respect. Children should not "fight it out" when they have a difference of opinion. Parents should teach children to consider both sides of every issue and resolve differences amicably.

Over the years this will build healthy respect for each other. It will teach you *not* to trust your physical strength or your ability to argue a case to win — right or wrong. It will prepare you for situations you will face outside our home during the remainder of your lives.

We must be able to love one another the way Jesus loves us. That love should be tested and expressed as we live in harmony with one another.

DISCUSSION QUESTIONS

Why is it still important to obey God's commandments?

When the Jewish religious leaders tried to snare Jesus by getting Him to say the commandments were no longer important, He responded by adding two new commandments. What are these two rules?

Can you give an example of a time when it was difficult for you to express love to someone?

Now give an example of a time when someone expressed love to you when you were acting unloving toward them. How did their love make you feel?

Unit 5

A Man Who Longed To Do God's Will

The life of David provides us with a wonderful example of a man who longed to please God, even though he made some very serious mistakes. He was genuinely sorry for his sins, and God loved him and forgave him.

God called David "a man after His own heart" (1 Sam. 13:14). That means David was the kind of man God loves in a special way. I believe it was David's genuine repentance that touched the heart of God. He did not take God's forgiveness lightly, as though God owed it to him. We do not read of his return to the same sins for which God had forgiven him.

God wants us to do His will so we will not have to experience the pain of disobedience. He will forgive our sins completely, just as He forgave

David's sins. Our enemy, Satan, tries to rob us of our joy by reminding us of our past failures. But we do not have to give him any "head room."

We can resist him. With humility we can say: "You are right! I did that. But you know I am forgiven. Jesus died for my sin, and my heart has been made clean."

He will flee if he sees he is defeated. This is a good time to use the same portions of the Word of God that David used to defeat Satan.

▶ Use the format on the following pages to lead your family in a responsive reading. Read David's affirmation aloud to your family. Ask them to respond by reading the "Our Response" section.

A Responsive Family Reading

David's Affirmation:

You have commanded us to keep Your precepts diligently (Ps. 119:4).

Our Response:

I want to keep Your commandments diligently.

David's Affirmation:

Blessed are those who keep Your testimonies and seek You with their whole heart (Ps. 119:2).

Our Response:

I want Your blessing, Father God. Help me seek You with my whole heart.

David's Affirmation:

I remember Your name in the night, O Lord (Ps. 119:55). I thought about my ways and turned my feet toward Your testimonies (Ps. 119:59).

Our Response:

Father God, I have thought about my ways, and I have turned my feet toward Your ways.

David's Affirmation:

Your word I have hidden in my heart, that I might not sin against You (Ps. 119:11).

Our Response:

Help me to remember the verses we have learned, as a reminder to do Your will when I am tempted to do wrong.

David's Affirmation:

Incline my heart to Your testimonies (Ps. 119:36).

Our Response:

Rule in my heart, Lord Jesus.

Pray this prayer with David:

Oh, that my ways were directed to keep Your statutes, then I would not be ashamed, when I look into all Your commandments (Ps. 119:6).

Weekly Participation Chart

Here are some instructions for using the sample chart on the next page to chart your family's progress through this devotional guide. You will need to make a copy of the chart for each week of study.

MEMORY VERSE COLUMN

Give one point for *almost* perfect attempts.

Give five points for the first perfect recitation.

Give two points for each day thereafter of perfect recitation.

OTHER COLUMN

Enter the total number of points earned for daily contributions.

Keep a scratch pad available during each daily session. Keep score for each child. Give one point for correct answers to questions. Give one point for each contribution the child makes during discussion times.

Establish monthly rewards for the highest scorer. A visit to McDonald's or to see a movie may be possibilities for monthly rewards. A trip to a nearby amusement park or an outing of the child's choice may work as a reward for the highest scorer at the end of the year.

WEEKLY PARTICIPATION CHART

WEEK _____

Date Completed _____

NAME	UNIT 1	UNIT 2	UNIT 3	UNIT 4	UNIT 5
	Memory	Memory	Memory	Memory	Memory
	Other	Other	Other	Other	Other
	Memory	Memory	Memory	Memory	Memory
	Other	Other	Other	Other	Other
	Memory	Memory	Memory	Memory	Memory
	Other	Other	Other	Other	Other
	Memory	Memory	Memory	Memory	Memory
	Other	Other	Other	Other	Other
	Memory	Memory	Memory	Memory	Memory
	Other	Other	Other	Other	Other

If you enjoyed *As for Me and My House*, we would like to recommend the following books:

Kids Are a Plus
by Ray Mossholder
In the same popular style of *Marriage Plus* and *Singles Plus*, Ray Mossholder offers practical guidance for parents in raising their children from birth through the teen years. Parents will discover ways to meet the challenges of living in a society that isn't always "kid-friendly."

Fifty-Six Days Ablaze
by Ron Luce
From Teen Mania, here's the teen power book for radical spiritual growth. This illustrated, eight-week devotional includes Bible memory verses, questions and answers, and frank discussions of the issues that teens face today including friends, music, church, prayer and more.

Available at your local Christian bookstore or from:

Creation House
600 Rinehart Road
Lake Mary, FL 32746
1-800-283-8494